Alyce Alexandra is the best-selling author of nine cookbooks for slow cookers and thermo cookers. She has her own range of kitchen accessories, runs her own cooking school and is the creator of alycealexandra.com, selling all things slow cooking, thermo cooking and kombucha.

Alyce is passionate about every avenue of food, from seedling to stomach. Her mission is to get people cooking, more often and from scratch, by showing how easy, achievable and rewarding home cooking can be. Her unpretentious, work-every-time recipes have made her a much-loved figure that people know and trust in the kitchen. She lives, gardens, writes, cooks and eats in Victoria, Australia.

alycealexandra.com
@alycealexandracookbooks
@alycealexandraxo

Also by Alyce Alexandra

Quick Fix in the Thermomix
Miniseries: Low Carb
Quick Fix Every Occasion
Miniseries: Super Healthy
Recipes from our Cooking School
Quick Dinners
Everyday Thermo Cooking
Thermo Cooker Fresh Favourites

Modern SLOW COOKER

alyce alexandra

VIKING
an imprint of
PENGUIN BOOKS

This book is dedicated to my sister Ellen,

for it was only possible because I had you by my side. xo

CONTENTS

SWEET TREATS

DRINKS

STAPLES

FRESH ACCOMPANIMENTS

INTRODUCTION

Of all the projects I've ever done, I see this book as perhaps the most important. Not even I could have anticipated how much this book would change my life – change how I view cooking – and I sincerely hope it will change yours too. What I realised, after cooking every single one of my meals in a slow cooker for nearly 6 months, is how calm this style of cooking is. And trust me, I wouldn't generally describe myself as calm! This is the cook I want to be, the person I want to be – this is how I envision my life. And the best bit is there's nothing aspirational about it! Armed with this book, anyone with a $50 slow cooker can cook delicious and nutritious food they are proud to serve and share. They'll be eating more healthily, more sustainably, saving money, saving time, caring for animals and stressing less! This really is life-changing stuff, and I couldn't be prouder of the blueprint I've created, which is as much for me as for you.

I care passionately about the importance of cooking from scratch. Small steps lead to big changes, and we get the opportunity to contribute positively three times every single day! I truly believe that the world would be a better place if everyone cooked a few more meals at home each week, but in today's busy society, cooking is often the first thing we outsource. While some may argue that this makes economic sense, the cost and benefit of doing so cannot be measured in dollars alone.

I am the first to admit that cooking can feel like a chore I've got to cram into my already busy day – I get the challenge! Takeaway and prepackaged food can be very appealing, I know. That's what first attracted me to the slow cooker – I saw how this appliance could take the hassle out of meals, meaning people would cook more often (and enjoy it!). But I soon realised that an appliance is nothing without the recipes to use it, like a smartphone with no apps. So I started creating the dishes in this book, ensuring first they were delicious but, just as importantly, that they were doable. Short ingredient lists, clear and concise instructions, beautiful photos to guide and inspire. Real recipes you will actually cook for you and your family . . . a modern makeover for the old slow cooker!

Home cooking does not need to be a finicky work of art – it can be a harmony of quality ingredients cooked simply (and slowly!). Anyone with a slow cooker, regardless of skill level or time constraints, can cook a delicious meal they are proud of. Serve it in the middle of the table, get the whole family sitting around, eat and enjoy. 'Simple yet satisfying' is my motto, and in today's world, simple is often exactly what we need. I have never aspired to be the greatest cook, but rather the greatest at inspiring others to cook. I believe the best way to do that is to make cooking approachable to all – with down-to-earth recipes and delicious results, people are hooked. I hope my cookbooks are the ones with crinkled pages covered in chocolate fingerprints and oil splatters. The ones that never make it onto the bookshelf in the living room as they are tucked safely in the kitchen.

Now, I'm not saying you can cook *everything* in a slow cooker – you certainly can't! I'm the first to acknowledge that. But for some things it's a game changer, and those are the recipes I've included in this book. If the slow cooker is brilliant at it, I've included it here. If it takes a bit of finessing, I've left it out. Simple as that. But don't tell me a slow cooker is only good for soups and stews! I've got salads, cheesecakes, puddings, pastas, tacos, sauces, curries, mash, cocktails, cordials, polenta chips, noodles and so much more. I've taken the slow cooker where

it's never gone before, and I know you're going to love it! Sure, you don't need a slow cooker – you could cook all these recipes on the stove or in the oven, in the same way that you don't need a kettle as you can boil water on the stove, and you don't need a toaster as you can grill bread in the oven. But I reckon a slow cooker might just change your life.

Lastly, let's talk meat-free cooking. Why? It's simple – because I love animals and I don't want to kill them. In today's world, we are lucky enough to have all the resources we need to eat a delicious and nutritiously balanced diet without meat . . . so why wouldn't we? Not to mention the health benefits and the environmental consider-ations. Growing food to feed food (as we often do for pigs, chickens, fish and cows) while many in the world are starving seems crazy to me! And who couldn't do with more veggies and fibre in their diet, anyway? But let me be clear, I'm not one for labels – every single plant-based meal someone chooses to eat is a win for me, no matter how they classify themselves. If this book inspires you to eat one less meal with meat a week, I see that as a victory. This book is for *everyone*, not just vegans and vegetarians. And, frankly, the slow cooker is great for veggies, fruit, legumes, beans, grains and pulses – so let's celebrate it!

Thank you for picking up this book, thank you for reading these words, thank you for caring about the food you eat and the earth we live on. This book is written with so much love from me to you – I really hope you use it and love it, and that your life is made just that little bit easier and more enjoyable along the way.

Happy cooking,

Love alyce xo

This isn't an aspirational coffee table book, this is a real cookbook – a helping hand to partner you in the kitchen. These are achievable recipes, made without fancy techniques or dexterity. I consider these recipes my shortcuts to living the good life, and I am so excited to share them with you.

WHY THE

slow cooker?

For me, one of life's biggest mysteries is why everyone doesn't use a slow cooker every single day! They are undoubtedly one of the handiest yet most underrated kitchen gadgets. Let me tell you why . . .

It literally could not get any easier. Dump and run – no checking, no monitoring, no stirring. Set and forget. *Everyone* can cook!

It frees up time. Slow cooking is by far the quickest form of cooking (in a roundabout way!), as once everything's in the pot you're free to not only manage something else in the kitchen but to leave the house entirely! Or sleep. Or do whatever you need to do. The slow cooker doesn't need you – spend your time doing something that brings you joy.

Meals are ready when you want them. Breakfast is ready to eat when you wake up in the morning, lunch is ready to be ladled hot into a food flask or thermos before heading out for the day, and dinner is ready to serve when you walk in the door at night. Even the speediest microwave meal (eek!) can't do that.

Your meals are healthy. Slow cookers cook on a low heat, which means the ingredients' nutrients are retained without any potentially carcinogenic burnt bits. High temperatures can cause a 30 per cent loss of the vitamin content of some vegetables, whereas cooking them low and slow preserves those nutrients. Not to mention your meals will be healthier simply by virtue of the fact that you cooked them yourself!

Your food has more flavour. Literally, as there's no evaporation of volatile compounds – all the flavours stay right in the pot. Vegetables taste sweeter slow cooked, while grains, beans and legumes cook to tender perfection and taste far superior than anything coming out of a can (which, let's be honest, is what we'd be using without a slow cooker).

You can't stuff it up. Slow cooking is incredibly forgiving! Where a stove or oven can take a dish from perfection to charcoal in a matter of minutes, a slow cooker isn't fazed if the phone rings right as you're due to serve it up. You couldn't stuff this up if you tried.

They're cheap to buy. You'll spend between $30 and $150, and you'll have your slow cooker for life! They really are very accessible. Want my tips on which one to buy? Head to page 9.

They're cheap to run. Slow cookers use much less power than other forms of cooking – just a little more energy than a traditional light bulb – making them good for your wallet and the environment. You'll also often be running them during the day, so you'll be using power at a low-demand (aka cheaper) time. They also won't heat up your kitchen in summer, so the air conditioner won't need a run either.

You can leave it on. Unlike the iron or hair straightener you're forever petrified you've left on, the slow cooker is perfectly fine to continue working its magic while you're out. For people who spend most of their day away from home, this feature cannot be overstated!

You can bulk cook. Most slow cooked food freezes really well, meaning you cook when you've got the time and energy, and when you don't, you heat up something delicious and nutritious from the freezer. To my mind, it's the ultimate way to run your kitchen – it's no more effort to cook 2 L of soup than one, so why not? Defrost and reheat it a month later, and you'll never feel like you're eating the same meal twice. It's almost like ordering takeaway, but without the cost, wait time and unhealthy ingredients, right? See page 20 for my freezing tips. All recipes in this book suitable for freezing are labelled as such.

Dirty dishes are kept to a minimum. Most of the time you're only dirtying your slow cooker insert, a chopping board and a knife . . . meaning there's barely any washing up (phew!). Sometimes you'll also need a frypan, and occasionally a food processor or blender, but really it's pretty low key. Fewer dishes equals more quality time with loved ones around the dinner table. Recipes that only use the slow cooker insert I call my 'one pot wonders', and these are labelled accordingly.

Your shopping bill will be low. Slow cookers generally do best with ingredients that are cheap to buy – root vegetables, apples, cooking tomatoes, dried lentils, beans, grains and pulses. Many of the recipes in this book will cost you around $10 to shop for and will feed six. Compare that to a quick sizzle-on-the-stove recipe and it seems cheap; compare that to ordering takeaway and you're laughing!

Whether you're a great cook or a novice, whether you love or hate cooking, the slow cooker will make your life a whole lot easier. You'll be saving money, reclaiming precious time, eating healthier and doing your bit for the environment. What's not to love? You just need the right recipes.

Slow cooker MYTHS

In order for me to bring the wonder of the slow cooker to the modern world, we need to bust some old slow cooker myths!

Slow cooker food is watery. Slow cooking requires a whole new way of thinking about food. You can't take a standard oven or stovetop recipe and expect it to work in a slow cooker – it is going to be watery! That's because, unlike most cooking methods, a slow cooker doesn't allow for any evaporation, so you need much less liquid than you would otherwise. Unless you're really confident with your slow cooker, stick to tried and tested recipes designed for a slow cooker – let me make the mistakes so you don't have to!

Slow cookers overcook vegetables. Here's the truth: slow cookers don't overcook vegetables, people overcook vegetables. Follow the times specified in this book and layer the ingredients exactly as I've specified and I promise – no overcooked veggies.

You only use a slow cooker for long cooking times. It's called a slow cooker, not a long cooker! There are so many great things you can do in an hour or two in your slow cooker, like chia puddings, mac 'n' cheese, corn salad, caramelised bananas and even my smoky pulled 'pork'! Sure, you could do those recipes in less time on the stove, but my view of 'quick and easy' is based on the hands-on time only. Being able to throw all the ingredients in, flick a switch and head out to the garden, take a shower, get some work done, pop to the shops or, better yet, sit down and really enjoy the company of those I'm about to eat with (game of cards, anyone?), and then come back an hour later to a perfectly cooked meal . . . that's my kind of quick and easy.

Slow cooked food tastes bland. I've got an easy answer for that: use better recipes! I promise this cookbook is filled with flavour. One thing people often notice when they start to cook from scratch using real, wholesome ingredients is how much salt you need to add to bring out all the flavours. Salt is a natural flavour enhancer. Ever made a curry with heaps of incredibly flavourful ingredients but it tastes bland? It simply needed more salt. When we cook with packet ingredients, ready-made sauces, etc., these ingredients are already filled with salt, so we don't realise how much of it we're actually eating and how much is needed to make food taste good. Buy a good-quality, unrefined salt and you'll be getting a nice dose of minerals along with your tasty meal.

Slow cookers are only good for meat. That's like saying a frypan is only good for steak! Being able to cook dried chickpeas and lentils from scratch while hardly giving it a thought – amazing. Being able to cook puddings and cheesecakes without the traditional set-up of an oven and water bath – game changer. Being able to infuse wines and ciders without burning off the alcohol – saviour!

You need to always have your slow cooker full. This just isn't the case – I commonly use my 6 L slow cooker only a quarter full and it's totally fine. I always say you're better off having a bigger slow cooker and using it only half- or a quarter-full most of the time, rather than having a smaller one with no option to increase the quantity for bulk cooking or entertaining. For all my slow cooker purchase tips, check out page 9.

Slow cookers don't cook food evenly. It is true that the ingredients at the bottom of the unit will cook more than those on the top, but we can use this to our advantage! We

don't necessarily want all our food cooked the same – the chickpeas and potatoes are definitely going to need more cooking than the tomatoes and zucchini, so we layer ingredients accordingly. That's why I often highlight the need to place ingredients in the slow cooker in a particular order.

Slow cookers are only good for soups and stews. What if I told you they could be used to cook baked cheesecake, fresh and zesty pearl barley salad, crispy fried mac 'n' cheese, foolproof coconut yoghurt, BBQ sauce, tacos and a sweet and spiced apple cider toddy? All recipes in this book, all recipes done in a slow cooker! That's what this book is all about – thinking differently about your slow cooker and seeing the many, many ways it can enrich your life (beyond soup and stew!). Dare I say it again – you just need the right recipes!

It's all about thinking differently about your slow cooker, and this book will have you doing just that – I'm so excited for you!

CHOOSING YOUR
slow cooker

Firstly, let's remember – every slow cooker slow cooks! I really don't want you stressing if you already have a slow cooker that doesn't match my recommendations. I wrote this book using six different slow cookers (often all at once!), and while they were all large units, some of them didn't meet my other preferences. Was it a little annoying? Yes. Did they all get the job done in the end? Absolutely. It has also made me extremely passionate and well-informed about what to recommend to you, so there's always a silver lining! So, if you're starting from scratch or you're committed to slow cooking multiple times per week and you're looking to purchase a new unit, then there's a few features that I highly recommend to make your life easier . . .

Bigger is better. All recipes in this book have been developed for a 5–6.5 L slow cooker. I recommend this size as it allows you the option of cooking in bulk. While most of the time you're probably not feeding that many people, most slow cooker meals freeze well and therefore it's great to make extra and store it in the freezer for super-quick homemade meals in the future without the mess (living the dream!). And remember, you don't have to fill it up every time you use it, it's fine being half- or even a quarter-full. The majority of recipes in this book do not even come close to using 5 L, but when I want to make more, the option is there – better to have it available than not. Also, for many of my recipes I place 500 ml preserving jars or 2 L pudding basins inside the slow cooker – you'll have a much easier time fitting these in a large unit. Of course, my recipes can easily be adjusted for smaller slow cookers – simply scale down the ingredients to fit in your unit. The cooking times will generally stay the same.

Invest in an electronic timer. If buying a new slow cooker, my second most important recommendation would be to buy a model with an in-built electronic timer, meaning the slow cooker will keep track of time for you. When your dish has finished the specified cooking time the unit will default to the 'keep warm' setting, keeping food hot for serving without overcooking it. This is especially handy for overnight cooking or a long day away from home. These units generally cost a little bit more, but I think the convenience and peace of mind are worth it. Of course, it's by no means essential – without a timer you will simply need to keep track of your cooking times yourself and manually turn to 'keep warm' if you're not ready to serve (and you'll need to make sure you're home on time!).

Make sure you've got control of the heat setting. Believe it or not, there are slow cookers out there that think they know better than you and 'automatically' set the temperature. I have one, and it is beyond frustrating! Make sure you can manually set the 'high', 'low' and 'keep warm' settings, meaning you can follow along precisely with the recipes in this book and get perfect results every time.

Make sure the minimum time setting is 30 minutes. Some models frustratingly have a minimum time setting of 4 hours – that may be minimum for your pot roast, but for many of the recipes in this book, we'll be cooking for less than 4 hours. So make sure the timer goes up in (at least) 30-minute increments. Again, I have one unit that starts at 4 hours and it drives me crazy – if you've already got one and are not planning to part with it, you'll simply need to set an alarm on your phone or oven to remind you of the actual time to turn the unit off.

Consider a searing slow cooker. Slow cooker inserts (the bowl inside the unit) are generally made of ceramic or enamel-coated metal. The benefits of a metal insert are threefold – they are much lighter than the ceramic inserts, they're much harder to break, and metal inserts often have a 'searing base'. This means you can put the slow cooker insert directly on the stove, sautéing onions and browning ingredients straight in your slow cooker, saving time, effort and dishes.* You can also reduce sauces down after your cooking is finished, if desired. Some high-end slow cookers even allow you to sauté inside the slow cooker itself, with a separate 'sear' function that is much hotter than standard slow cooker settings. Alternatively, you will need to do these tasks in a frypan and then transfer the contents to your slow cooker, which isn't a huge problem, but it is one more pan to wash up. My caution with metal inserts is that it is very easy to scratch the non-stick coating, so you must ensure to never use metal utensils in your slow cooker – I recommend only silicone. You may also want to investigate what the non-stick coating is made from, as this will be in sustained contact with your food.

*Please only put your slow cooker insert directly on heat if your model specifically advertises that it is made for that purpose – not all metal inserts are!

And that, my friend, is the lowdown on slow cookers.

SLOW COOKER
Tips and Tricks

You'll be slow cooking like a pro after these little nuggets of wisdom . . .

No sudden changes in temperature. Number-one rule – never fill a cold slow cooker insert with boiling hot liquid or fill a hot insert with cold liquid. The sudden change of temperature may result in damage (including breakage!) of the slow cooker insert. This happens most when people serve their meal out of the hot slow cooker and then add cold tap water straight away to soak the insert before cleaning.

Don't lift the lid until the cooking is done. I totally get the temptation to check on your masterpiece, but unless a recipe explicitly tells you to do something that requires the lid to be removed before the cooking is finished, leave the lid in place! This really is one of the most important rules, as lifting the lid drastically drops the temperature inside the slow cooker, extending the cooking time and throwing your recipe off. If you (or someone else in the house!) does lift the lid accidently, I would add an extra 15 minutes to the total cooking time. And don't worry – where a recipe calls for you to add ingredients part way through cooking, I have factored in this loss of heat.

Give everything a really good stir, unless the recipe says otherwise. There are times you're going to open the slow cooker and go, 'Oh fudge, this hasn't worked,' and then after a good stir you'll be thinking 'OMG that looks delicious!' Most of the time after a long cook everything is going to need a good mix, folding the contents at the bottom of the slow cooker to the top and so forth. This is not just a token swirl through! I will always specify in my recipes when I want you to give everything a good stir, and the importance of this step cannot be overstated. Conversely, there are a few times when you definitely should *not* stir. On such occasions I've explicitly noted this in the method. It's not just an 'oh, you don't need to worry about it' situation, it's that we want to preserve the layering of ingredients in the slow cooker.

Sauté your onions, always. Never add onions to a slow cooker dish that you haven't sautéed first – I find you get that slight raw onion flavour throughout and it just ruins the dish for me. I really think it's worth the extra effort (and it's particularly easy if you have a searing slow cooker).

It's easy to double recipes, just do the maths. If you've got a large slow cooker, many of the recipes in this book can easily be doubled. You'll need to think about it for a second though – if you've got a 6 L slow cooker and my nourishing Asian broth calls for 3.5 L of water, this isn't one of those recipes. However, you'll have plenty of room for a double batch of my lazy tacos, which need a total of 6 cups (1.5 L) of ingredients. Scale your ingredients accordingly, and follow exactly the same method and cooking time.

You can halve recipes, to a point. If you're only feeding one or two people and you don't have a love affair with your freezer like I do, then you may want to halve some recipes. For the most part this isn't a problem – just scale down the ingredients and follow exactly the same method and cooking time. However, you can only get away with this to a point – you always want the base of the slow cooker completely covered with ingredients. The other issue is if the recipe calls for a stick blender – if you don't have enough ingredients in the slow cooker and you start whizzing them with a stick blender you'll end up wearing half the food as it sprays up everywhere! In this case, you'll need to transfer the slow cooker contents to a jug or

small saucepan and blitz it up that way, or use a blender or food processor.

Use oil if food is sticking. I've never found the need to do this, but if food is sticking to your slow cooker insert, give it a brush with olive oil before adding in your ingredients. If sticking food is a big problem, I'd suggest that the coating on your slow cooker insert is damaged, possibly through scratches or general wear and tear. You can often buy replacement slow cooker inserts without buying a whole new unit, so that might be a good option for you.

Use the right utensils. Don't ever use metal in your slow cooker – it's not worth the risk of possible damage to your insert. Wooden or plastic utensils are totally fine, but my pick is silicone – naturally non-stick, hygienic and no chance of scratches. My silicone spatula is available from alycealexandra.com.

If you don't like dishes, get a stick blender. A stick blender is nowhere near as powerful or effective as a good blender or food processor, but still, I just love the convenience of it – using your stick blender straight in the slow cooker insert means no faffing about transferring hot liquid, and much less washing up at the end. They're between $30 and $150, and if you're serious about slow cooking I would suggest investing in one.

Don't convert your own recipes. But if you do, think carefully about liquid content. In a slow cooker, as the moisture evaporates, rather than escaping as it would in other cooking techniques, it gently drips back down from the lid into the food. This means the liquid requirement of a slow cooker recipe is much, much lower than anything done on the stove or in the oven . . . and often when people try to convert their family-favourite recipes to the slow cooker it's this part they get wrong (meaning watery dishes!). Stick to specially designed slow cooker recipes – let me make the mistakes so you don't have to!

Cooking times are loose, unless I explicitly state otherwise. The cooking time for my harissa-spiced creamy carrot soup is 4 hours on high or 8 hours on low, but honestly, if you left it on for 5 hours on high or 10 hours on low, it wouldn't be that big a deal. And if it ticked over to 'keep warm' for 2 hours before you pureed it, that also wouldn't matter so much. I'm not saying be totally flippant with timing! But it's not like baking things in an oven. There are, of course, some exceptions, and these usually involve pasta. Where precise cooking times are important, I've explicitly noted that in the recipe. When you see this, set the timer on your phone and pay attention! Otherwise, don't stress.

Don't fill your slow cooker right to the top. Filling the slow cooker within an inch of its life may mean that you get some bubbling overspill, and a mess down the front of your slow cooker and onto the bench. Always leave at least 3 cm space at the top of your slow cooker. If you're using a 6 L slow cooker and the recipes in this book, this will never be a consideration, but if you're using a smaller unit or scaling up recipes it's something to be mindful of.

You can do some bits ahead of time. For speedy mornings, you can sauté your onion and other ingredients the night before and refrigerate them, dumping them in your slow cooker in the morning. You can also chop your veggies and store them in the fridge, and you can measure out your spices. The only thing I wouldn't prepare in advance is anything to do with dry, starchy ingredients such as flour, oats, lentils, beans or pasta.

Cook in advance. At a guess, I'd say 80 per cent of the recipes in this book actually taste better in the days after they're cooked, rather than being eaten straight away! So if it's convenient, cook your meal a day or two in advance and simply reheat when ready to serve. Soups, stews, ragus, curries . . . they'll all benefit from this. Even many of the recipes containing pickled ingredients like salads and fresh accompaniments fall into this category. The only exceptions are pasta and porridge – these are best eaten as soon as they're ready.

Safety first. Be aware that the metal casing on the outside of the slow cooker gets really hot, and will absolutely burn you if touched. Keep your hands off the outside and always use oven mitts when removing a hot slow cooker insert. Please make sure your slow cooker is somewhere that little hands cannot reach. It's also a good idea to give it space. Given your slow cooker can get really hot during use, make sure not to position it hard up against walls or cabinets to avoid potential damage.

Cleaning 101. Only ever wash the slow cooker insert. Nnever submerge the base/casing of the slow cooker in water – it should only ever need a wipe down with a damp cloth. Wash the insert in hot soapy water, first soaking it if it looks like it needs it. Don't use an abrasive scourer that could damage the coating. Most inserts are dishwasher proof (just check the manual first), however I find if you wash it quickly or soak it then it's super easy to clean and doesn't need to take up precious space in the dishwasher.

As every slow cooker is different, I recommend reading the manufacturer's instructions for your particular model before use. Never use your slow cooker contrary to the manual. Ensure that your slow cooker is suitable for use directly on heat source (such as stove) before using it in this manner.

THE SLOW COOKER *pantry*

To make cooking easy and fuss-free, it is essential to have a well-stocked pantry – this cannot be overstated! Whether you are pulling together a meal for that evening before leaving for work, trying to find something for the lunchboxes you can slow cook overnight or simply want to put on a sweet treat that evening, having the basics on hand will mean that a nourishing and delicious morsel cooked from scratch is never far away. In fact, some of the recipes in this book require nothing more than a handful of pantry staples! It may take a little investment at the beginning, but the long-term benefits more than make up for it as you will be saving time and money by buying quality ingredients in bulk and whipping up meals without even leaving the house to shop. Frankly, if I had to shop for every ingredient in a recipe every time I wanted to cook something, that would be enough to put me off too!

I keep my pantry items in stackable BPA-free plastic containers with airtight lids, each with a clearly visible label on the front. It's important that the containers are transparent so you can quickly gauge which items are running low without needing to open them. I love the idea of glass jars, but I find these can get quite heavy when full, making it difficult to carry several ingredients at once! And they often aren't stackable. I keep my everyday staples such as olive oil, balsamic vinegar, salt and faux-chicken stock powder (page 184) out on the countertop so they're always in easy reach when cooking.

Turn over for my essential slow cooker pantry list . . .

Oil/Vinegar

- Extra virgin olive oil*
- Balsamic vinegar
- Apple cider vinegar

Fruits/Vegetables

- Canned coconut cream
- Canned coconut milk
- Tomato passata**
- Tomato paste
- Shredded coconut
- Vanilla beans
- Brown onions
- Garlic

Sweeteners

- Caster sugar
- Brown sugar
- Honey
- Maple syrup
- Golden syrup

Sauces

- Worcestershire sauce
- Harissa paste
- Red miso paste
- Tamari
- Smooth peanut butter

Herbs/Spices

- Curry powder
- Mexican spice mix (page 185)
- Mixed spice
- Sweet paprika
- Smoked paprika
- Ground cinnamon
- Ground cumin
- Ground cardamom
- Ground turmeric
- Whole star anise
- Whole cinnamon sticks
- Whole cloves
- Whole cumin seeds
- Whole fennel seeds

Nuts/Seeds

- Raw cashews
- Chia seeds
- Sesame seeds

Grains

- Basmati rice
- Plain flour
- Cornflour
- Dried macaroni pasta
- Rolled oats
- Udon noodles

Beans/Legumes

- Dried chickpeas
- Dried green lentils
- Canned four bean mix

Other

- Faux-chicken stock powder (page 184)
- Baking powder
- Bicarbonate of soda
- Vanilla extract
- Cocoa powder

- Nutritional yeast flakes
- Fine salt
- Soy milk

The following items are not essential, but if we're going for 'ultimate pantry' set-up I would also recommend . . .

- Pine nuts
- Slivered almonds
- Flaxseeds
- Dried penne pasta
- Pearl barley
- Split red lentils
- White miso paste
- Rosewater
- Liquid smoke
- Pitted dates
- Currants

And there's a few kitchen products that I couldn't do without when slow cooking . . .

- 2 L non-stick pudding basin with lid
- 500 ml preserving jars with lids
- 250 ml preserving jars with lids
- Silicone spoon spatula
- Fine mesh strainer
- Stick blender***
- High-powered blender, food processor or thermo cooker

*If you're in Australia, buy Australian grown and pressed extra virgin olive oil, and use it within 6 months of opening. European olive oil is amazing, if you're in Europe.

**Buy jars of tomato passata or make your own (page 167)! You can store homemade passata in the pantry, providing you run it through a preserving unit first. Alternatively, you can freeze it.

***If you've got a high-powered blender, food processor or thermo cooker, strictly speaking you then don't need a stick blender too, but I do love being able to put the stick blender straight into the slow cooker, saving time and minimising dishes.

THE FACTS
on freezing

Even before I was obsessed with slow cooking, I was obsessed with my freezer! It just seems like such a no-brainer to me to make a bit extra and freeze it – shop, cook and wash dishes once, enjoy a delicious, nutritious, homecooked meal multiple times. And did I mention how much money you save?! I get that not everyone is happy eating the same meal twice in a row, but once it's been in the freezer for a couple of weeks or months, the original meal is well forgotten. I see my freezer the same way others see Uber Eats! When I'm tired, lacking motivation or low on time, I turn to the freezer and see what I can defrost for dinner.

The slow cooker and the freezer make the perfect pair because it's so easy to cook in bulk with your slow cooker, enjoying a warm meal straight away, and squirrelling some into the freezer for another day. But in order to turn your freezer into the local take-away directory I have a few tips . . .

You must label everything. Don't put anything in the freezer without a date and a label, no exceptions. You think you'll remember it's that delicious smoky Moroccan stew that you made on 5 June? You won't. And then you'll be scared of it, and it'll get ignored in the back of the freezer for all eternity. Have a dedicated section in your freezer for ready-made meals and have everything in there well labelled. Then it will be a joy to browse through and pick tonight's dinner.

Stick to shallow plastic. When freezing soups, stews, curries, poached fruit and other 'wet' dishes, I always stick to plastic containers to avoid the possibility of broken glass, as water expands when frozen. Shallow containers are the best choice as it makes it easier to remove the frozen block when you're ready to reheat, especially if you didn't have time to defrost first.

The smaller the container, the better. Freeze meals in portions that you and your family will eat in one sitting. Then you can simply defrost the amount you want, not the whole batch! If in doubt, you're better off freezing things in multiple small containers rather than one large container.

Plan ahead. Ideally, pull out your frozen dinner the night before, or that morning, and put it in the fridge. By dinner time your meal should be defrosted and ready to reheat – this saves time and makes reheating easy.

Special notes for freezing in glass jars . . . There are quite a few recipes in the Staples chapter of this book where I cook in jars inside the slow cooker. This saves time, makes life easy and ensures even cooking, and what's even more convenient is being able to throw these jars in the freezer. It can be done!

There a just a few extra rules:

- Avoid jars with 'shoulders' – you want jars that have straight sides all the way up, rather than tapering in at the top.
- Always leave at least 3 cm empty space in the top of the jar. This allows for the fact that water expands when it freezes.
- Refrigerate the jars before freezing – don't just go from warm jars on the bench straight to the freezer.
- Don't screw the lid on too tightly – loosely lidded is fine. Once the contents is frozen it won't be spilling anywhere!

The majority of recipes in this book are suitable for freezing! And in fact, often soups, stews and curries taste better a few days after they've been cooked. So it's not just convenience, it's also better flavour. Look out for the 'freezer friendly' tag throughout this book.

Best RECIPES FOR . . .

Loading up the freezer

- Spicy lemongrass and lentil soup (page 77)
- Super-simple passata (page 167)
- Rhubarb and strawberry compote (page 37)
- Pumpkin soup with a kick (page 63)
- Spicy Thai red curry (page 104)

Reheating leftovers

- Thick and saucy veg bolognese (page 81)
- Harissa-spiced creamy carrot soup (page 53)
- Mexican bean taco bowls (page 50)

Not missing the meat

- Smoky pulled 'pork' (page 110)
- Ultimate vegan lasagna (page 102)
- BBQ baked beans (page 45)

A lighter meal

- Clean green soup (page 73)
- Nourishing Asian broth (page 61)
- Saucy silken tofu (page 69)
- Spiced Indian beetroot (page 65)

Feeding a crowd

- Creamy potato and pea massaman (page 82)
- Easy Indian chana masala (page 91)
- Smoky Moroccan stew (page 94)

A lazy weekend brunch

- Deluxe caramelised banana breakfast pudding (page 40)
- Saucy shakshouka (page 33)

A hangover cure

- Crispy fried mac 'n' cheese (page 92)
- Fast-food nachos (page 105)

Taking to a summer picnic

- Jazzy Mexican corn salad (page 118)
- Tangy Asian barley salad (page 70)
- Cheat's 'baked' cheesecakes (page 136)

Your Friday night lazy dinner

- Lazy tacos (page 55)
- Easiest jacket potatoes (page 76)
- Go-to simple and satisfying tomato pasta (page 58)
- Two-minute chicken noodles (page 109)
- Caramelised rum bananas (page 146)

Packing into lunchboxes

- Fresh and zesty pearl barley salad (page 120)
- Ultimate lemony zucchini pasta (page 67)
- Loryn's spiced lentil salad (page 126)

A romantic meal

- Saucy vodka pasta (page 106)
- Self-saucing molten chocolate pudding (page 134)
- Sweet and spiced apple cider toddy (page 151)

Quick mid-week breakfast

- Creamy coconut porridge (page 32)
- Super-simple everyday chia breakfast (page 43)

Enjoying around a fire

- Boozy hot choccy (page 157)
- Proper chai (page 158)
- Classic spiced mulled wine (page 161)

Edible gifting

- Chilli and fennel seed infused oil (page 181)
- No-joke hot sauce (page 175)
- The best BBQ sauce (page 169)

A fancy dinner party

- Celebration quince syrup (page 159)
- Middle Eastern eggplant and lentils (page 97)
- Rolls-Royce hummus (page 130)
- Sticky date pudding for everyone (page 139)
- Cheat's gooey caramel sauce (page 173)

HOW TO COOK
seasonally

To me, eating seasonally is a no-brainer – even without the altruistic benefits, it is such a win for the individual. The cheapest, freshest, healthiest, best-tasting produce is always whatever's in season. When else in life can you get the best quality at the lowest price? It's also the most environmentally friendly and sustainable option, as you'll be eating food that's been grown locally, travelled minimal food miles, and has not spent months in cold storage. The food is also likely to require fewer herbicides and pesticides in the growing, meaning fewer chemicals end up on your plate (and in our waterways).

My best advice for knowing what's in season in your area at any given time is to head to a local farmer's market and see what they're selling. If everyone's got plenty of zucchinis on offer at a good price, then that's what you should be eating! They will have been grown recently, locally and probably utilising proper crop-rotation practices (again, fewer chemicals). You'll often find what's available at the local market and the big supermarket differs vastly. Co-ops and online organic delivery services are also a great way to access local, seasonal, usually organic fresh produce.

As a keen home gardener, I can tell you there are plenty of nuances to seasonality that a simple chart cannot capture, but I will try! Your location plays a massive part, as does the weather that season and the seasons prior. Technically, you can grow broccoli year-round in Victoria, but if you've ever tried it in the warmer months, you'd know the cabbage butterflies are so unrelenting that to get any edible broccoli you'd need to heavily spray your crop with pesticides . . . so instead we simply grow it in the cooler months when there are no butterflies around. It's all about working with nature, not against it.

Autumn produce
Fig
Kiwifruit
Mushroom
Parsnip
Persimmon
Plum
Pomegranate
Pumpkin
Quince
Raspberries
Rhubarb
Squash
Sweet potato
Tamarillo
Tomato

Winter produce
Apple
Avocado
Broccoli
Brussels sprouts
Carrot
Cumquat
Kohlrabi
Leek
Mandarin
Nashi
Orange
Pear
Rosemary
Salad greens
Silverbeet
Tangelo

Spring produce
Asparagus
Basil
Beans
Beetroot
Cabbage
Cauliflower
Coriander
Cucumber
Garlic
Grapefruit
Kale
Lemon
Lime
Onion
Peas
Radish
Spinach
Zucchini

Summer produce
Apricot
Berries
Cantaloupe
Capsicum
Cherries
Chilli
Corn
Eggplant
Grapes
Lychee
Mango
Nectarine
Parsley
Passionfruit
Peach
Pineapple
Watermelon

Autumn recipes
Raspberry breakfast compote (page 47)
Celebration quince syrup (page 159)
Fresh and zesty pearl barley salad (page 120)
Magic pasta sauce jars (page 179)
Ultimate vegan lasagna (page 102)
Smoky Moroccan stew (page 94)
Super-simple passata (page 167)
Thick and saucy veg bolognese (page 81)

Winter recipes
Balsamic brussels sprouts (page 129)
Creamy cauli and leek soup (page 57)
Satay laksa (page 87)
Thick and chunky minestrone soup (page 88)
Perfectly poached pears (page 39)
Harissa-spiced creamy carrot soup (page 53)
Tuscan white bean and rosemary soup (page 75)

Spring recipes
Clean green soup (page 73)
Rhubarb and strawberry compote (page 37)
Spiced Indian beetroot (page 65)
Toasty rosemary potatoes (page 119)
Ultimate lemony zucchini pasta (page 67)
Jazzy Mexican corn salad (page 118)
Garlicky spit pea dahl (page 83)

Summer recipes
'Canned' beetroot slices (page 183)
Creamy mango coconut pudding (page 145)
Middle Eastern eggplant and lentils (page 97)
No-joke hot sauce (page 175)
Saucy shakshouka (page 33)
Tropical mango coulis (page 174)
Mexican bean taco bowls (page 50)

This list is simply a guide, getting you thinking about the seasonality of your cooking. Plenty of recipes in this book span multiple seasons (some even year-round!), so please do not think that because a particular recipe or ingredient is not listed here, it's not in season. Again, what people in your area are growing (particularly in their backyards!) is going to be a much better indicator than anything I can write.

THE important STUFF

Slow cooker. These recipes have been written using slow cookers with a minimum capacity of 5 L. If yours is smaller, no problem! You can still cook all the recipes, but you might need to scale down some of them to fit, while others will be just fine as they only fill half a large slow cooker.

Teaspoons. I use Australian metric measurements, meaning 1 teaspoon = 5 ml and 1 tablespoon = 20 ml.

Oven. All oven temperatures are for a fan-forced setting unless otherwise stated. My experience is that oven temperatures can vary dramatically, so I recommend you get to know your own oven and adjust the temperatures accordingly. You may also need to rotate baking trays during the cooking time to ensure even cooking and browning.

Weights. The weight specified for each ingredient is after the ingredient has been prepared as per instruction (for example, pumpkin, peeled, seeds removed). Please factor this in when shopping.

Dietary requirements. If you or the people you are cooking for have any dietary requirements, make sure you check your ingredients carefully for allergens or foods they are avoiding. For example, the cream I buy doesn't contain gelatine, but many brands use it as a thickener, meaning that recipe is no longer vegetarian. Also, a surprising number of what you'd consider basic ingredients like spice mixes contain gluten as a filler. So always check the ingredients list on the package!

I want to make sure everyone can eat nutritious, tasty food no matter their dietary requirements and preferences, so you'll find that lots of the recipes in this book are already free of many common allergens and animal products or can be easily varied to make them so . . .

For recipes catering for specific dietary requirements look for the following:

+dairy free
No ingredients containing dairy, including milk, cheese and butter

+vegan
Contains no animal products at all, including meat, dairy, eggs and honey

+egg free
No eggs present, or ingredients containing egg

+nut free
No nuts, including peanuts, macadamias and nut milks

+soy free
No ingredients containing soy, including tofu

+gluten free
No ingredients containing gluten

Where any of these tags has (option) written next to it, this means you should look for the option I give to adapt this recipe for different dietary requirements. These are usually written below the recipe in a note like this.*

*For a gluten-free option, try . . .

For other recipe features, look for the following:

+freezer friendly
Freezes well to be eaten later

+one pot wonder
Just what it sounds like – minimal washing-up required! All cooking done in your slow cooker insert.

Most of these recipes require a few minutes of preparation in the evening, but then you get to wake up to a nourishing hot breakfast ready to enjoy straight away – which I think is a pretty good deal! You're probably going to use the 'low' temperature setting for these recipes to stretch out the cooking times while you sleep, but I reckon my saucy shakshouka (page 33) and BBQ baked beans (page 45) also make great lunch options, so the high setting might come in handy to put it on when you wake up and have lunch ready to serve 4 hours later. A couple of recipes, such as my everyday chia pudding (page 43), only need an hour in the slow cooker – I put these on first thing when I wake up, then go and get ready for the day, coming back to a warm brekkie right before I walk out the door. Whatever is easiest for you, I've got you covered. Also convenient is that, once a recipe is cooked, individual family members can serve up their portion whenever they like, while the slow cooker happily sits on the 'keep warm' function. Nourishing, real food, while factoring in the realities of life.

breakfast

Creamy
COCONUT PORRIDGE

1 ripe banana

400 g can coconut milk

1 cup (90 g) rolled oats*

200 ml water

¼ cup (20 g) shredded
coconut

¼ cup (55 g) brown sugar

Pinch of salt

EXTRAS

2 L pudding basin or
small casserole dish
(preferably with lid)
that fits inside slow
cooker

Serves 2
Hands-on time: 5 mins
Total slow cooker time:
3 or 6 hours

This recipe is perfect for putting on before bed and enjoying first thing in the morning. What makes it even easier is investing in a slow cooker with a digital timer – once the cooking time is up the slow cooker will keep breakfast warm for whenever you are ready (without risk of overcooking). The banana/coconut/oats combo makes this one seriously satisfying (and delicious!) breakfast . . . you won't be looking for morning tea!

FIRST

1. Place banana and coconut milk in pudding basin or casserole dish, roughly mashing with a fork to combine. Add remaining ingredients and stir through well. Cover with lid or foil, sealing tightly.

2. Place inside slow cooker, then add water until the dish is two-thirds submerged. Cover and cook for 3 hours on high or 6 hours on low (this recipe doesn't do well if it keeps cooking – best if you've got a programmable slow cooker that will tick over to keep warm after the allocated time).

3 OR 6 HOURS LATER

3. Stir porridge for a minute, until creamy and thick.

Serve with maple syrup, cinnamon, extra brown sugar, cream, yoghurt, chopped nuts, stewed fruit or fresh berries . . . the options are endless!

When cooking in a slow cooker, you never want instant oats! Always use traditional rolled oats.

Tip: If the porridge is a little too thick for your liking, add a splash of boiling water and stir through – this will thin it out beautifully.

+one pot wonder +dairy free +vegan +egg free +nut free +soy free

SAUCY
shakshouka

- 2 large capsicums, thinly sliced*
- 500 g very ripe tomatoes, diced
- 4 garlic cloves, diced
- ½ cup (150 g) sun-dried tomatoes (including their oil), diced
- 2 tablespoons harissa paste**
- 2 tablespoons tomato paste
- 1 teaspoon smoked paprika
- 1 teaspoon sweet paprika
- 2 chicken-style stock cubes or 1 tablespoon faux-chicken stock powder (page 184)
- 1 medium Desiree potato, peeled and grated
- 4 free-range eggs
- Fine or flaked salt

Don't ask me to properly pronounce shakshouka, but it is one of my favourite breakfasts! A rich and flavoursome tomato sauce with perfectly poached eggs on top . . . all done in the slow cooker. Simple, yet oh so satisfying. Always buy free-range eggs and check the stocking density on the box – anything over 1,500 birds per hectare (or worse, stocking density not listed!) is not free range in my book. I'm the proud mum of 12 beautiful hens, and I can assure you, chickens are no different than cats and dogs. They have big personalities, love to give and need lots of care – after all, those little bodies give us a nutritious, protein-laden eggs most days. Healthy, happy chickens equal healthy, happy eggs!

FIRST

1. Place capsicum, tomatoes, garlic, sun-dried tomatoes, harissa paste, tomato paste, smoked paprika, sweet paprika and stock cubes or stock powder in slow cooker. Stir to combine. Cover and cook for 4 hours on high or 8 hours on low.

4 OR 8 HOURS LATER

2. Add grated potato and give everything a really good stir. Make four wells in the top of the tomato mixture and crack in eggs. Give everything a sprinkle with salt.

3. Cook on high for 15 minutes or until eggs are cooked to your liking. 15 minutes should give a runny yolk, whereas 25 minutes should get a firm yolk.

Spoon out portions of tomato mixture topped with an egg. Serve garnished with zhug (page 196), salsa verde (page 197), fresh parsley, fresh chives, grated cheese, labne or za'atar and a slice of hot, buttered sourdough or Turkish bread. *Recipe continued over page >*

Serves 4
Hands-on time: 15 mins
Total slow cooker time:
4 ¼ or 8 ½ hours

RECIPE CONTINUED

If possible, use one red and one yellow capsicum.

**Harissa paste is a concentrated fiery concoction made from blended peppers, oil and spices. While it is traditionally used in North African and Middle Eastern cooking, I find a small amount does great things for almost any cuisine. I always have a jar in the fridge! I add a teaspoon or two to any dish that needs a flavour boost, including pasta sauces, ragus, curries, roast vegetables, tagines, soups, noodle dishes, couscous and risottos. You can even stir the paste through mayonnaise or Greek yoghurt to make a dipping sauce or dressing. Make your own or purchase from delis in jars or tubes.*

Tip: Ditch the eggs from this recipe and simply cook through the potato at step 3 (this thickens the sauce) and you've got yourself a delicious vegan breakfast. Serve with toast and garnish with fresh herbs and toasted pine nuts.

RHUBARB *and* STRAWBERRY COMPOTE

1 bunch rhubarb, cut into
   3 cm pieces

500 g strawberries,
   hulled*

1 cup (220 g) brown sugar

1 vanilla bean, halved
   lengthways

2 tablespoons chia
   seeds**

Serves 6
Hands-on time: 5 mins
Total slow cooker time:
2 ½ or 5 hours + 15 mins
standing

I have a thriving rhubarb patch that lets me harvest year-round, so this recipe is one of my go-tos – it's a brilliant base for whatever sweet breakfast or dessert I fancy. A little sweet from the strawberries, a little sour from the rhubarb, it's one of my favourite combinations. But of course if you've got an apple that's looking a little soft or some other berries that need using, throw them in too. The more the merrier! I always say it's not about recipes that are perfect for me, it's about what you like and what you have on hand. So make your own!

FIRST

1. Place rhubarb, strawberries, sugar and vanilla bean in slow cooker. Cover and cook for 2 ½ hours on high or 5 hours on low.

2 ½ OR 5 HOURS LATER

2. Add chia seeds. Stir until everything is well combined. The chia seeds will swell and thicken everything up so don't stress if it looks a little watery at this point. Allow to stand for 15 minutes before serving (so the chia can work its magic). If you can find the vanilla bean, fish it out.

Delicious served warm or cold with porridge, granola or yoghurt, or used as a base for a crumble or strudel – you can make a delicious breakfast crumble using coconut oil, nuts and oats! Also makes a great accompaniment to desserts, especially if you're looking for something not too sweet. Or simply serve with a scoop of ice cream!

*Frozen strawberries work perfectly well for this recipe and are often easier to get in the cooler months. If using, add straight to slow cooker (still frozen) and increase cooking time to 3 hours on high or 6 hours on low.

**Chia seeds are little black or white seeds that are great for digestive health (use either type for this recipe). Available from health food stores or supermarkets.

breakfast

+freezer friendly +one pot wonder +dairy free +vegan +egg free +nut free +soy free +gluten free

Perfectly
POACHED PEARS

8 firm but ripe brown
  pears, peeled

1 ½ cups (330 g) caster
  sugar

10 cm knob ginger,
  finely grated or
  1 vanilla bean,
  halved lengthways

6 cups (1.5 L) water

1 lemon, juiced

Serves 8
Hands-on time: 10 mins
Total slow cooker time:
3 or 6 hours

Whole pears, perfectly poached in a ginger or vanilla syrup, looking pretty as a picture when served. I love the combination of sweet pears and spicy ginger, but I appreciate not everyone's a fan, so I have also done a variation with vanilla. I love that these pears stay firm even when cooked (I promised no mushy food!) and also won't discolour at all, even after days in the fridge. So, make a batch on the weekend and they'll get you through breakfasts (and dessert!) for the week.

FIRST

1. Place all ingredients in slow cooker, submerging pears as much as possible. If you can't fully submerge them, add extra water. If the pears float up, weigh down with a metal trivet or a saucer. Cover and cook for 3 hours on high or 6 hours on low.

3 OR 6 HOURS LATER

Pears are ready! Perfect served warm or cold with granola, pancakes, porridge or yoghurt for breakfast, but easily makes the transition to dessert when accompanied by cream, ice cream, custard or rice pudding. The leftover liquid can be reduced in a saucepan to make a delicious syrup or bottled up, refrigerated and used to poach your pears or apples next time. This usually keeps in the fridge for about a month.

Tip: You may want to pour poaching liquid through a fine mesh strainer to remove the bits of ginger.

breakfast

+freezer friendly +one pot wonder +dairy free +vegan +egg free +nut free +soy free +gluten free

DELUXE CARAMELISED BANANA
breakfast pudding

1 cup (170 g) chia seeds

2 × 400 ml cans coconut milk

2 teaspoons ground cinnamon

3 ripe bananas, cut into 5 mm slices

¼ cup (55 g) brown sugar

3 teaspoons butter*

½ cup (70 g) slivered almonds

Natural coconut yoghurt, to serve**

Serves 5
Hands-on time: 15 mins
Total slow cooker time: 1 hour

This is not your standard running-out-the-door weekday breakfast – this is pretty special and perfect for a lazy Sunday morning. There are a couple of steps involving a frypan, but all in all it won't take you more than 15 minutes hands-on time to pull together . . . in fact I think it's got a great effort-to-impressiveness ratio. Put the slow cooker on as soon as you wake up and by the time you're showered and dressed with a coffee in hand it'll be ready for the next step. If you really want to hurry up the total time, fry your almonds and banana while the slow cooker is on, meaning at the 1-hour mark you can serve it all up straight away. Note here – don't just make the chia pudding part and skip the toppings, this is not the recipe for that! The sweetness and flavour comes from the caramelised banana. If it's a simple chia pudding you're after, head to page 43.

FIRST

1. Place chia seeds, coconut milk and cinnamon in slow cooker. Stir to combine. Cook on high for 1 hour.

1 HOUR LATER

2. Toss banana slices in brown sugar until evenly coated. Set aside.

3. Heat 1 teaspoon butter in a large frypan over medium heat. Once hot, add almonds and stir frequently until golden, about 5 minutes. Don't leave the stove as they'll burn easily. Once golden, immediately tip out onto a plate.

4. Return pan to the heat and add remaining 2 teaspoons butter. Once melted, add sugar-coated bananas. Cook until just starting to become golden, about 3 minutes. You do not want to burn the sugar – turn the heat down if necessary.

+dairy free (option) +vegan (option) +egg free +soy free +gluten free

Divide chia puddings between five serving bowls. Top with a dollop of coconut yoghurt, caramelised bananas and a sprinkling of toasted almonds. Perfection!

Use a plant-based butter for a vegan and dairy-free option.

**Natural coconut yoghurt is simply the original unsweetened, unflavoured version. You can make your own! My foolproof recipe is on page 171.*

foolproof
coconut yoghurt
(page 171)

Super-simple
EVERYDAY
CHIA
BREAKFAST

1 cup (170 g) chia seeds*

2 × 400 g cans coconut milk

¼ cup (80 g) jam or coulis**

1 teaspoon finely grated orange or lemon zest (optional)

Serves 5
Hands-on time: 5 mins
Total slow cooker time: 1 hour

I really love chia seeds for breakfast – they're filling (meaning I'm not left looking for a mid-morning snack!), easy to prepare and, when combined with the right ingredients, super delicious! Here I've used coconut milk for a rich and creamy texture without the dairy, and jam, which gives a delightful flavour along with a touch of sweetness. Want an apricot chia pudding? Use apricot jam! The touch of zest adds a nice citrus hint, and given how often orange and lemon skins end up in the compost (or worse, the bin) after being eaten or juiced, it's really a free ingredient, so if you've got some, throw it in. This is my favourite type of recipe – one guideline, endless possibilities. Enjoy!

FIRST

1. Place chia seeds, coconut milk, jam and orange zest (if using) in slow cooker. Stir to combine. Cook on high for 1 hour.

1 HOUR LATER

2. Give everything a really good stir, evenly distributing jam.

Breakfast is ready! Top with yoghurt (page 177), coconut yoghurt (page 171), fresh fruit, toasted nuts, shredded coconut or poached rhubarb and strawberries (page 37). If you're not feeding five, decant into glass jars, refrigerate and enjoy as chilled chia puddings throughout the week – portable instant breakfast!

Chia seeds are little black or white seeds that are great for digestive health (use either type for this recipe). Available from health food stores or supermarkets.

**Use any flavour jam or coulis you like! My favourite jams are peach, raspberry or apricot, or try my rose-berry coulis (page 180) or tropical mango coulis (page 174).*

+one pot wonder +dairy free +vegan +egg free +nut free +soy free +gluten free

BBQ
baked beans

2 tablespoons extra virgin olive oil

1 brown onion, diced

4 garlic cloves, diced

2 × 400 g cans cannellini beans or four bean mix

1 potato, peeled and grated

¼ cup (90 g) golden syrup

¼ cup (60 ml) Worcestershire sauce*

2 tablespoons Dijon mustard

3 chicken-style stock cubes or 1 ½ tablespoons faux-chicken stock powder (page 184)

2 teaspoons smoked paprika**

1 kg ripe tomatoes, diced

Serves 5
Hands-on time: 15 mins
Total slow cooker time:
4 or 8 hours

Saucy, smoky, slightly sweet . . . these are the ultimate 'baked' beans. They're known predominantly as breakfast fare, but really, I can't see why these beans aren't perfect for lunch, dinner, sides or snacks! On toast, with fried eggs, in a burrito, with roast vegetables or in a food flask for a toasty warm lunch on the go. I really wish I could have written the recipe to use dried beans rather than canned, but the reality is the slow cooker doesn't do so well with dried kidney-shaped beans – they really need to be cooked first. So, if you've got a bit of time, cook your own beans from dried (you'll need 1 cup of dried beans to equal 2 cans' worth), but if not, the canned option works wonderfully.

FIRST

1. Heat oil in a large frypan over medium heat. Once hot, add onion and sauté for 5–10 minutes or until soft. Add garlic and continue cooking for a couple of minutes. Transfer to slow cooker.

2. Add beans, potato, golden syrup, Worcestershire sauce, mustard, stock cubes or stock powder, smoked paprika and tomato. Stir to combine. Cover and cook for 4 hours on high or 8 hours on low.

4 OR 8 HOURS LATER

3. Give everything a really good stir and you're ready to go!

Serve with toast, cheese and possibly some fresh greens and herbs, or keep in the slow cooker on the keep warm setting for as long as needed. If you're after a sleep-in, a slow cooker with an electric timer makes this a breeze.

For this recipe to be vegetarian and vegan, use an anchovy-free Worcestershire sauce. There are heaps of recipes on the internet showing you how to make your own!

**I like my beans really smoky, so I'd add an extra teaspoon of smoked paprika, but for kids or my smoke-averse sister Loryn, I'd leave it out. You could always use sweet paprika instead.*

+freezer friendly +dairy free +vegan +egg free +nut free +soy free +gluten free

RASPBERRY BREAKFAST COMPOTE

4 sweet apples, cored
  and cut into 8
  wedges*

1 lemon, juice only

500 g frozen raspberries

2 tablespoons chia
  seeds**

Serves 6
Hands-on time: 10 mins
Total slow cooker time:
3 or 6 hours + 15 mins
standing

Simple stewed fruit ready for breakfast, without any added sugar –
just the delicious sweetness from the apples! And the nutrients and
fibre from the chia seeds (but don't worry, no one but you will know
they're in there). A slow cooker with a timer is great for this one so
it's ready and on the keep warm function when you wake up, but
really it's just as good cooked on the weekend and served up cold
throughout the week. Of course, you can use any variety of berries
for this recipe – I just love the pretty pink hue the raspberries offer.

FIRST

1. Place apples and lemon juice in slow cooker, stir to combine,
ensuring all apple slices are coated in lemon juice. Add raspberries,
stir again to combine. Cover and cook for 3 hours on high or
6 hours on low.

3 OR 6 HOURS LATER

2. Add chia seeds and stir to combine. The chia seeds will swell
and thicken so don't stress if it looks a little watery at this point.
Allow to stand for 15 minutes before serving (time for the chia to
work its magic).

Delicious served warm or cold with porridge, granola or yoghurt, or
used as a base to a crumble or strudel – you can make a delicious
breakfast crumble using coconut oil, nuts and oats! Also makes a great
accompaniment to desserts, especially if you're looking for something
not too sweet. Or simply serve with a scoop of ice cream!

*I like gala apples for this recipe, but any sweet apple will work perfectly. If you want to
use a cooking apple such as Granny Smith, you'll want to add in a little sugar at step 1.*

**Chia seeds are little black or white seeds that are great for digestive health (use either
type for this recipe). Available from health food stores or supermarkets.*

breakfast

+freezer friendly +one pot wonder +dairy free +vegan +egg free +nut free +soy free +gluten free

Despite its reputation, the slow cooker is just as apt for fresh and light dishes as it is hearty and comforting ones! In this chapter we've got light pastas, fresh Mexican dishes, bright soups and salads, Asian broths and more. And the slow cooker is definitely not just for winter cooking – in fact, I think it really shines in the warmer months. No need to crank up the oven or stand over a hot stove because the slow cooker undemandingly ticks away on the bench without heating up the whole kitchen. It's the time I'd most like to be outside, enjoying the garden and the sunshine, not spending hours in the kitchen. And as the sun goes down, I venture back to the house with a smile, knowing there's a big pot of delicious lemony zucchini pasta (page 67) waiting for me.

fresh and light

MEXICAN BEAN
taco bowls

1 cup (200 g) green lentils, rinsed

1 red capsicum, diced

1 yellow capsicum, diced

500 g ripe tomatoes, diced

1 cup (160 g) frozen corn kernels

2 × 400 g cans four bean mix, rinsed and drained

1 tablespoon golden syrup

4 tablespoons Mexican spice mix (page 185)*

1 chicken-style stock cube or 2 teaspoons faux-chicken stock powder (page 184)

¼ cup (60 ml) Worcestershire sauce**

700 g passata***

Tortilla chips, to serve

This might just be one of my favourite recipes in this book . . . it takes literally 10 minutes of hands-on time to make, most of the ingredients I routinely have on hand, there are hardly any dishes, you can tailor everyone's bowl to their personal taste and preference, and it freezes well! Oh, and did I mention it's seriously tasty? The first time I made this recipe I served it to my dad and sister Loryn for lunch (the two fussiest eaters in the family!) and both of them were fighting for seconds . . . I knew I was onto a winner.

FIRST

1. In this order, place lentils, capsicums, tomatoes, corn, beans, golden syrup, spice mix, stock cube or stock powder, Worcestershire sauce and passata in slow cooker. Cover and cook for 4 hours on high or 8 hours on low.

4 OR 8 HOURS LATER

2. Give everything a really good stir, and you're ready to go!

Divide between serving bowls and top with your favourite toppings. Add a big handful of tortilla chips on the side.

+freezer friendly +one pot wonder +dairy free (option) +vegan (option) +egg free +nut free +soy free +gluten free

Toppings, to serve

Salsa verde
(page 197), pineapple
salsa (page 195), hot
sauce (page 175),
raita (page 192),
guacamole, tomato
salsa, cheese, sour
cream, pickled
jalapeños, shredded
lettuce, shredded
cabbage

Serves 6
Hands-on time: 5 mins
Total slow cooker time:
4 or 8 hours

If you don't have time to make your own, you can purchase a premade Mexican spice mix. Look for one without fillers and sugar. The one I buy contains garlic, chilli, cumin, onion, sweet paprika, black pepper, salt, oregano and parsley — nothing else.

**For this recipe to be vegetarian and vegan, look for an anchovy-free Worcestershire sauce, or better yet, make your own!*

***See page 167 if you want to make your own.*

Harissa-spiced CREAMY CARROT SOUP

¼ cup (60 ml) extra virgin olive oil

1 brown onion, diced

4 garlic cloves, diced

6 carrots (about 700 g), ends trimmed and cut into fifths

3 chicken-style stock cubes or 6 teaspoons faux-chicken stock powder (page 184)

2 tablespoons harissa paste

4 cups (1 L) water

400 ml can coconut cream

Serves 4
Hands-on time: 20 mins
Total slow cooker time: 4 or 8 hours

I had a few lacklustre responses to 'carrot soup' when I first created this recipe, but one taste successfully converted them all! It's sweet thanks to the carrots, subtly spiced thanks to the harissa and creamy thanks to the coconut. Plus a good dose of flavour thrown in in the form of garlic, onion and my famous faux-chicken stock powder. And those plus a little olive oil are, literally, all the ingredients – it couldn't be simpler.

FIRST

1. Heat oil in a large frypan over medium heat. Once hot, add onion and sauté for 5–10 minutes or until soft. Add garlic and continue cooking for a couple of minutes. Transfer to slow cooker.

2. Add carrots, stock cubes or stock powder, harissa paste, water and coconut cream. Cover and cook for 4 hours on high or 8 hours on low.

4 OR 8 HOURS LATER

3. Puree using a stick blender, food processor or blender until smooth (if using a blender or food processor you will need to do this in batches).

Ladle into bowls or keep warm in your slow cooker until ready to serve. Garnish not essential, but delicious topped with fried pine nuts, fresh herbs, zhug (page 196) and coconut yoghurt (page 171).

+freezer friendly +dairy free +vegan +egg free +nut free +soy free +gluten free

LAZY TACOS

2 cups (400 g) green
    lentils, rinsed

2 chicken-style stock
    cubes or 1 tablespoon
    faux-chicken stock
    powder (page 184)

3 cups (750 ml) water

400 g can diced
    tomatoes

1 tablespoon extra virgin
    olive oil

¼ cup (60g) sliced
    pickled chilli*

4 tablespoons Mexican
    spice mix (page 185)**

Taco shells, to serve

Toppings, to serve

    Salsa verde
    (page 197), pineapple
    salsa (page 195), hot
    sauce (page 175), raita
    (page 192), coleslaw,
    tomato salsa, corn
    kernels, shredded
    cheese, sour cream,
    pickled jalapeños,
    shredded lettuce,
    diced tomatoes

There really couldn't be a better recipe than this one when you're looking for a satisfying meal the whole family will enjoy while doing the least work possible! Also handy is that all the slow cooker ingredients are things I keep on hand in the pantry, meaning in a pinch I can always get the taco filling on in the morning, giving me the rest of the day to pick up tacos and toppings.

FIRST

1. Place lentils, stock cubes or powder, water, tomatoes, oil, chilli and spice mix in slow cooker, stir to combine. Cover and cook for 4 hours on high or 8 hours on low.

4 OR 8 HOURS LATER

Give everything a good stir and you're ready to start building your tacos! How easy was that?

Jars of pickled chilli are available from supermarkets and delis – most readily available are sliced pickled jalapeños, but any chilli will work.

**If you don't have time to make your own, you can purchase a premade Mexican spice mix. Look for one without fillers and sugar. The one I buy contains garlic, chilli, cumin, onion, sweet paprika, black pepper, salt, oregano and parsley – nothing else.*

Serves 6
Hands-on time: 5 mins
Total slow cooker time:
4 or 8 hours

CREAMY CAULI
and leek soup

2 tablespoons extra virgin olive oil

2 leeks, white part only, thinly sliced

2 cauliflower heads, including stalks, roughly chopped

4 chicken-style stock cubes or 2 tablespoons faux-chicken stock powder (page 184)

6 cups (1.5 L) water

400 ml can coconut cream

⅓ cup (20 g) nutritional yeast flakes*

2 teaspoons fine salt

Serves 6
Hands-on time: 20 mins
Total slow cooker time: 4 or 8 hours

I often debate whether to include ingredients in a recipe that need sautéing – do we really need to dirty that frypan?! I love cooking, but geez I hate washing up. In this case, however, I confidently stand by the leek – it adds so much flavour, and by sautéing it for a full 10 minutes we are really allowing those flavours to develop and shine. If all you can get is onions, use two of those instead, but the leek is where the magic is at. Also magical is the fact that, thanks to the coconut cream and nutritional yeast flakes, this soup is incredibly creamy and cheesy yet contains no dairy . . . at all! I promise you won't detect a hint of coconut!

FIRST

1. Heat oil in a large frypan over medium heat. Once hot, add leeks and sauté for 10 minutes or until soft. Transfer to slow cooker.

2. Add cauliflower, stock cubes or stock powder, water, coconut cream, nutritional yeast flakes and salt to slow cooker. Stir to combine. Cover and cook for 4 hours on high or 8 hours on low.

4 OR 8 HOURS LATER

3. Puree using a stick blender, food processor or blender until smooth (if using a blender or food processor you will need to do this in batches).

Ladle into bowls or keep warm in your slow cooker until ready to serve. Garnish not essential, but delicious sprinkled with shredded cheese, fresh parsley or chilli flakes.

Nutritional yeast, commonly referred to as 'nooch', is not the same as instant yeast used in bread baking or brewer's yeast. It's a flaky yellow powder that has a cheesy, umami flavour and is packed with B12 and other vitamins and minerals. Available from health food stores and some supermarkets.

+freezer friendly +dairy free +vegan +egg free +nut free +soy free +gluten free

Go-to simple and satisfying
TOMATO PASTA

¼ cup (60 ml) extra virgin olive oil

1 brown onion, thinly sliced

4 garlic cloves, diced

1 kg ripe tomatoes, diced*

1 cup (150 g) pitted kalamata olives**

1–2 red chillies, diced (optional)

2 chicken-style stock cubes or 1 tablespoon faux-chicken style stock powder (page 184)

2 teaspoons fine salt

2 tablespoons balsamic vinegar

2 cups (500 ml) water

500 g penne pasta

This is my go-to dinner – it's easy, it's tasty and I'm yet to find a person who doesn't like it! It's a simple tomato and olive pasta sauce cooked low and slow to make it extra sweet and delicious, but then we add the dry pasta straight to the slow cooker and it sucks up all those beautiful sauce flavours and releases starch, giving the sauce a little extra body as it cooks . . . it's marvellous. Simple, satisfying and oh so easy – no extra pot to monitor or wash. I think this recipe will be making a regular appearance in your kitchen!

FIRST

1. Heat oil in a large frypan over medium heat. Once hot, add onion and sauté for 5–10 minutes or until soft. Add garlic and continue cooking for a couple of minutes. Transfer to slow cooker.

2. Add tomatoes, olives, chilli, stock cubes or stock powder, salt, vinegar and water. Cover and cook for 4 hours on high or 8 hours on low.

4 OR 8 HOURS LATER

3. Give everything a really good stir. Add pasta, pushing down with the back of a spatula if necessary, ensuring that it is fully submerged. Cover and cook for 40 minutes on high (this is one of those times you need to be exact with time or you'll overcook your pasta).

4. Give it another good stir and test your pasta – it should be cooked al dente, but if not, cook on high for a further 10 minutes.

Serve your pasta straight away – don't leave in the slow cooker on the keep warm setting. Delicious as is, but happily garnished with cheese, parsley, basil, rocket leaves and perhaps an extra drizzle of olive oil.

+dairy free +vegan +egg free +nut free +soy free

Serves 4
Hands-on time: 15 mins
Total slow cooker time:
4 hours 40 mins or
8 hours 40 mins

*I always like using fresh tomatoes rather than canned, for flavour, health and environment, but if canned is all you've got absolutely use them – the recipe will work just fine (use 2 × 400 g cans diced tomatoes and half a cup of water).

**I know some people don't like olives! Easy – just leave them out. However, you might need to add a little extra salt before serving.

Nourishing
ASIAN BROTH

2 garlic cloves, peeled

3 cm knob ginger, thinly sliced

½ lemon, sliced

10 cloves

1 cinnamon stick, roughly broken

4 star anise, roughly broken

1 teaspoon fennel seeds

3 teaspoons fine salt

2 spring onions, white ends and green tops thinly sliced

3.5 L water

¼ cup (70 g) miso paste*

⅓ cup (80 ml) tamari**

1 tablespoon maple syrup

Serves 8
Hands-on time: 10 mins
Total slow cooker time:
6 or 12 hours

This is the recipe for when your digestion needs a little break, or you're wanting something light and healthy. The modern version of chicken soup for the soul. The broth is flavoursome and nourishing, especially after its long simmering time. This recipe makes a lot, perfect for bottling and freezing, meaning you can pull out a batch whenever it calls you and add whatever veggies and noodles you like – it's like a whole new recipe every time.

FIRST

1. Place garlic, ginger, lemon, cloves, cinnamon, star anise, fennel seeds, salt, white part of the spring onion and water in slow cooker. Cover and cook for 6 hours on high or 12 hours on low.

6 OR 12 HOURS LATER

2. Add miso, tamari and maple syrup. Stir until miso is dissolved.

3. Pour liquid through a mesh strainer to remove all chunky ingredients, leaving a clear broth. Discard solids.

Your broth is now ready! Add cooked noodles, bok choy, sliced mushrooms, Chinese cabbage and beansprouts for a hearty noodle soup, or seaweed and tofu for a simple miso soup. Garnish with thinly sliced spring onion tops and sesame seeds.

*If avoiding gluten and soy, ensure miso paste is gluten and soy free – it's hard to find but it can be done! Any type is fine for this recipe.

**Tamari is similar to soy sauce, although it is gluten free. It has a stronger, more complex flavour and is my pick for Asian dishes, but you can use soy sauce instead. Available from Asian grocers and health food stores. If avoiding soy, use a coconut aminos instead.

+freezer friendly +one pot wonder +dairy free +vegan +egg free +nut free +soy free (option) +gluten free (option)

PUMPKIN SOUP *with a kick*

2 tablespoons extra virgin olive oil

2 brown onions, diced

6 cm knob ginger, peeled and diced

6 garlic cloves, diced

2 long red chillies, diced

2 kg pumpkin, peeled and roughly chopped (4 cm pieces)

400 ml can coconut cream

¼ cup (30 g) curry powder*

2 chicken-style stock cubes or 1 tablespoon faux-chicken stock powder (page 184)

1 tablespoon fine salt

3 cups (750 ml) water

Serves 6
Hands-on time: 20 mins
Total slow cooker time:
4 or 8 hours

Everything you know and love about pumpkin soup, with the warming flavours of ginger, chilli and curry powder added for oomph. This soup's got big flavour! Make it in autumn when pumpkins are at their seasonal peak, meaning they're at their best and cheapest (wins all around). Load up the freezer and enjoy throughout winter. I wrote a similar recipe for a curried pumpkin soup on my blog back in 2012 (that one's done in the thermo cooker), and every year since it's been one of my most popular posts, so I know we've got the thumbs up!

FIRST

1. Heat oil in a large frypan over medium heat. Once hot, add onion and sauté for 5–10 minutes or until soft. Add ginger, garlic and chilli, continue cooking for a couple of minutes.

2. In this order, place pumpkin, onion mixture, coconut cream, curry powder, stock cubes or stock powder, salt and water in slow cooker. Cover and cook for 4 hours on high or 8 hours on low.

4 OR 8 HOURS LATER

3. Puree using a stick blender, food processor or blender until smooth (if using a blender or food processor you will need to do this in batches). Give it a really good puree – you want it silky smooth with a sweetness coming through. A high-powered blender is going to do the best job.

Ladle into bowls or keep warm in your slow cooker until ready to serve. Garnish not essential, but delicious topped with coconut yoghurt or crème fraîche.

*We are relying on the curry powder to bring big flavour to this recipe – invest in a good-quality one from a delicatessen or specialty food store.

lively apple and mint chutney (page 193) →

fresh yoghurt raita (page 192)

Spiced INDIAN BEETROOT

3 long green chillies, quartered*

4 garlic cloves, peeled

4 cm knob ginger, peeled

⅓ cup (80 ml) extra virgin olive oil

1 ½ teaspoons fine salt

2 teaspoons fennel seeds

2 teaspoons cumin seeds

1 teaspoon ground turmeric

½ teaspoon whole cardamom seeds

1 lime, zest finely grated, juiced

⅓ cup (80 ml) water

750 g beetroot, washed and cut into 2 cm cubes

2 cups (150 g) shredded coconut

½ cup (80 g) sultanas

Steamed rice, to serve

Cubes of beetroot cooked to tender perfection, tossed in a heavily spiced, super-flavoursome shredded coconut mix with plenty of lime zest for freshness. This recipe is what I describe as a fresh and light 'dry curry', very different to the stereotypical slow cooker meal in a rich gravy. At first glance it may look like a vegetable accompaniment, but it's so full of flavour it really holds its own as centre-stage dish, especially with fluffy white rice to soak up the spicy turmeric oil.

FIRST

1. Place chilli, garlic, ginger, oil, salt, fennel seeds, cumin seeds, turmeric, cardamom seeds, lime zest and juice and water in blender or food processor. Blend until pureed – it doesn't need to be smooth, just finely chopped. Spread across base of slow cooker.

2. Top with beetroot and shredded coconut. Stir everything to combine well. Cover and cook for 4 hours on high or 8 hours on low.

4 OR 8 HOURS LATER

3. Add sultanas, give everything a good stir.

For a complete meal, serve beetroot with fluffy steamed rice topped with a dollop of coconut yoghurt, fresh coriander, toasted sesame seeds, roasted cashews, raita (page 192), zhug (page 196) or apple and mint chutney (page 193). Also makes a great side dish at your next Indian banquet.

This dish is quite spicy – decrease the amount of chilli if that doesn't appeal to you!

Serves 4
Hands-on time: 15 mins
Total slow cooker time:
4 or 8 hours

fresh and light

+one pot wonder +dairy free +vegan +egg free +nut free +soy free +gluten free

Ultimate lemony ZUCCHINI PASTA

¼ cup (60 ml) extra virgin olive oil

1 kg zucchini, ends trimmed, roughly chopped into 2 cm pieces

4 chicken-style stock cubes or 2 tablespoons faux-chicken stock powder (page 184)

2 garlic cloves, diced

1 lemon, zest finely grated, juiced

500 g rigatoni pasta*

Serves 4
Hands-on time: 10 mins
Total slow cooker time: 8 hours 5 mins

I can feel your hesitation already – the ingredients list is scarily short and zucchini doesn't usually elicit excitement, but I promise this recipe is so surprisingly delicious (not to mention simple!) you'll be coming back again and again. After a (very) long slow cook, almost magically, this recipe turns into a rich and creamy ragu – a far cry from pale and watery zucchini! Combine that with a subtle hint of garlic and a decent whack of zesty lemon and you've got one very tasty yet still very fresh meal. Pair with a glass of sparkling rosé and I'm in heaven.

FIRST

1. Place oil, zucchini, stock cubes or stock powder and garlic in slow cooker. Cover and cook for 8 hours on high. Give it a really good stir at some point during the second half of the cooking time, breaking up the zucchini.

8 HOURS LATER

2. Cook pasta according to package instructions, however, drain it just before it's done, when it needs 30 more seconds.

3. Add lemon zest and juice to slow cooker. Give everything a really good stir, breaking up zucchini – don't worry if it's still a little bit watery at this point, the pasta will suck that up. Add in almost-cooked pasta and stir to combine. Cover and cook for a further 5 minutes on high (no longer or the pasta will be overcooked).

And you're ready to serve! Delicious as is, but optional yummy garnishes include fresh basil, fresh rocket, shaved parmesan, feta, chilli flakes, chilli and fennel seed infused oil (page 181), toasted pine nuts, vincotto or a balsamic reduction.

Use a gluten-free pasta for a gluten-free option. I really like buckwheat spirals.

fresh and light

+dairy free +vegan +egg free +nut free +soy free +gluten free (option)

crunchy crushed
cucumber salad
(page 191)

Saucy
SILKEN TOFU

- 1 cup (40 g) dried sliced shiitake or porcini mushrooms
- 3 cm knob ginger, finely grated
- 2 garlic cloves, diced
- 600 g silken tofu, drained and cubed
- 2 teaspoons brown sugar
- 1 teaspoon Chinese five spice powder
- ½ cup (125 ml) mirin
- ¼ cup (60 ml) tamari*
- ¼ cup (60 ml) black vinegar**
- 2 tablespoons toasted sesame oil***
- Steamed rice or steamed Asian greens, to serve

Serves 4
Hands-on time: 10 mins
Total slow cooker time: 3 or 6 hours

Soft, silky tofu (it lives up to its name!) with a delicious Asian sauce – the perfect balance of a little sweet, a little sour and a little salty. You could also add a sliced red chilli to make it a little spicy! The dried mushrooms will reconstitute over the long cooking time and also add big flavour to the sauce – it's a win-win. Best served over fluffy white rice so not a drop is wasted.

FIRST

1. Spread mushrooms evenly across base of slow cooker. Top with ginger and garlic, then cubed tofu, then sugar and five spice powder. Pour over mirin, tamari, vinegar and sesame oil. Don't try to stir – you'll break up the tofu. Cover and cook for 3 hours on high or 6 hours on low.

3 OR 6 HOURS LATER

Divide fluffy steamed rice or steamed Asian greens between serving bowls. Top with tofu, mushrooms and plenty of sauce. Be careful when spooning out – the tofu will be fragile; I find a large salad serving spoon works best. Sprinkle with toasted sesame seeds, toasted spring onions or fresh coriander. Serve with a side of cucumber salad (page 191).

Tamari is similar to soy sauce, although it is gluten free. It has a stronger, more complex flavour and is my pick for Asian dishes, but you can use soy sauce instead. Available from Asian grocers and health food stores.

**Black vinegar, also known as Chinese black vinegar, is a rich and complex vinegar with a touch of umami flavour. I love using it in Asian cooking, and it's my pick for a dipping sauce with dumplings. Available from supermarkets and Asian grocers.*

***Toasted sesame oil, a mellower version of pure sesame oil, is available from health food shops. If you can't get your hands on some, use 2 teaspoons pure sesame oil and 1½ tablespoons olive oil instead.*

+one pot wonder +dairy free +vegan +egg free +nut free +gluten free

Tangy Asian BARLEY SALAD

1 cup (200 g) pearl barley, rinsed

4 cups (1 L) water

3 teaspoons fine salt

2 red shallots, thinly sliced

1 red chilli, thinly sliced

4 cm knob ginger, finely grated

1 lime, zest finely grated, juiced

¼ cup (60 ml) rice wine vinegar or apple cider vinegar

1 tablespoon caster sugar

2 tablespoons toasted sesame oil*

2 lebanese cucumbers, cubed

1 mango, cubed**

Handful mint leaves

¼ cup (35 g) sesame seeds, toasted***

¼ cup (20 g) fried shallots****

We've got all the elements in this salad – shallots, ginger and chilli pickled in lime juice for a salty, spicy, sour flavour, fresh mint leaves and cucumber, sweet mango, crunchy fried shallots, toasty sesame seeds and fluffy pearl barley to soak up all that deliciousness! I think this salad holds its own as a meal, but of course you can serve it as a side with other Asian fare. Great in lunches on the go, as it's best served at room temperature.

FIRST

1. Place barley, water and 1 teaspoon salt in slow cooker. Stir to combine. Cover and cook for 3 ½ hours on high or 7 hours on low.

2. Meanwhile, in a large mixing bowl, combine shallots, chilli, ginger, lime zest and juice, vinegar, sugar and 1 teaspoon salt. Set aside to marinate while barley is cooking.

3 ½ OR 7 HOURS LATER

3. Drain excess water from barley and, ideally, allow to cool for 30 minutes.

4. Add barley to shallot mixture, along with oil, cucumber, mango, mint, sesame seeds, fried shallots and remaining 1 teaspoon salt. Toss until well combined.

Serve at room temperature or chilled. Just as good the next day, but hold off adding the fried shallots until just prior to serving so they retain their crunch. Garnish with extra mint leaves.

+one pot wonder +dairy free +vegan +egg free +nut free +soy free

Serves 4

Hands-on time: 15 mins

Total slow cooker time: 3 ½ or 7 hours

*Toasted sesame oil, a mellower version of pure sesame oil, is available from health food shops. If you can't get your hands on some, use extra virgin olive oil instead.

**If you can't get mango, use pineapple or canned lychees. You want something tropical, fresh and sweet! Failing that, dice up a green apple.

***To toast sesame seeds, heat a frypan over medium heat. Once hot, add sesame seeds and continually stir or toss. Don't leave the stove as they'll burn very quickly! Once they start to colour, immediately remove from the heat – the residual heat from the pan will do the rest of the job.

****Fried shallots are dried and packed in bags or plastic tubs. They're available from supermarkets or Asian grocers and will keep for a couple of months in the pantry.

Clean green SOUP

2 cups (240 g) frozen peas

4 chicken-style stock cubes or 2 tablespoons faux-chicken stock powder (page 184)

2 cups (160 g) finely shredded green cabbage

100 g green beans, cut into 2 cm pieces

1 lemon, zest finely grated, juiced

1 red chilli, thinly sliced

6 cups (1.5 L) water

Handful mint leaves

Serves 4
Hands-on time: 10 mins
Total slow cooker time: 2 or 4 hours

This is a light, refreshing broth that's also warming and nurturing . . . the perfect combination when you feel your digestive system needs a night off! The lemon, chilli and mint ensure we've got plenty of flavour, while the veggies are lightly cooked, still retaining their crunch – the only way to do cabbage in soup in my opinion. Now, the world's your oyster with this recipe – use whatever green veggies you like and have on hand. Do a fridge clean-out and see what odds and ends you can chuck in. I've gone for the cabbage and green bean combo, but feel free to use finely chopped silver beet, kale, zucchini, broccoli, spinach or even brussels sprouts!

FIRST

1. Place peas, stock cubes or stock powder, cabbage, green beans, lemon zest, chilli and water in slow cooker. Stir to combine. Cover and cook for 2 hours on high or 4 hours on low.

2 OR 4 HOURS LATER

2. Add mint leaves and lemon juice, give everything a good stir.

Ladle your soup into bowls or a food flask for later. Garnish not needed, but fresh herbs such as parsley or basil are delicious, as are grated cheese or chilli flakes. Pictured is my cheesy herb sprinkle – tasty cheese, basil, mint, salt and garlic all whizzed up together.

Tip: To bulk up this recipe, add a can of beans (rinsed and drained) at step 1 – my pick would be cannellini beans.

+freezer friendly +one pot wonder +dairy free +vegan +egg free +nut free +soy free +gluten free

TUSCAN WHITE BEAN
and rosemary soup

¼ cup (60 ml) extra virgin olive oil

3 garlic cloves, peeled

2 fresh bay leaves

2 rosemary sprigs

1 teaspoon fine salt

1 chicken-style stock cube or 2 teaspoons faux-chicken stock powder (page 184)

3 × 400 g cans cannellini beans, rinsed and drained*

4 cups (1 L) unsweetened almond milk

Serves 5
Hands-on time: 10 mins
Total slow cooker time:
4 or 8 hours

I first had the pleasure of a dish comprising olive oil, garlic, fresh rosemary, almonds and cannellini beans on a trip to Italy, and since then I've been in love with the combination – not just because it reminds me of lunch on a picturesque Tuscan hillside! Here I've blended them all into a silky soup, which is luscious but still surprisingly fresh. The slow cooker means we can really extract all the flavours from the rosemary and bay leaf – I highly recommend growing your own as they're incredibly hardy and two of the easiest edibles to grow. If you've got the space, it's always easier planting directly in the ground, but they'll also be very happy in pots, provided they get watered enough. And then you've always got a sprig or two to throw into your cooking, without effort, waste or expense.

FIRST

1. Place oil, garlic, bay leaves, rosemary, salt, stock cube or stock powder, cannellini beans and almond milk in slow cooker. Cover and cook for 4 hours on high or 8 hours on low.

4 OR 8 HOURS LATER

2. Remove bay leaves and rosemary sprigs. Puree using a stick blender, food processor or blender until smooth (if using a blender or food processor you will need to do this in batches).

Ladle into bowls or keep warm in your slow cooker until ready to serve. Serve drizzled with truffle oil or chilli and fennel seed infused oil (page 181) and a thick slice of buttered toast (preferably olive bread).

I've used canned beans for convenience, but ideally cook your own cannellini beans for this recipe (more flavour, healthier and better for the environment). You'll need 1 ½ cups (300 g) dried cannellini beans, and they'll need to be soaked overnight and then simmered for 1 to 1 ½ hours, so get started on this recipe early!

fresh and light

+freezer friendly +one pot wonder +dairy free +vegan +egg free +soy free +gluten free

EASIEST
jacket potatoes

4 large potatoes,
scrubbed and dried*

4 teaspoons extra virgin
olive oil

Salt flakes

Toppings, to serve

Zhug (page 196),
salsa verde (page 197)
beans, chilli, ragu,
curry, coleslaw,
tomato salsa, corn
kernels, cheese,
sour cream, pickled
jalapeños, shredded
lettuce

EXTRAS

4 squares of foil

Serves 4
Hands-on time: 5 mins
Total slow cooker time:
4 or 8 hours

Let me level with you here – these jacket potatoes won't have the crispy skin you get from an oven, however they'll be fluffy, moist and perfectly cooked inside, and they'll be ready the minute you walk in the door! So, I reckon it's a fair exchange (it's the only way I now cook my jacket potatoes!).

FIRST

1. Prick each potato multiple times with a fork and place on a square of foil. Drizzle each with 1 teaspoon oil and sprinkle with salt. Wrap each tightly in foil.

2. Arrange potatoes in a single layer on bottom of slow cooker (it's okay if they are packed tightly). Cover and cook for 4 hours on high or 8 hours on low.

4 OR 8 HOURS LATER

Your jacket potatoes are ready to serve! Unwrap foil and cut a cross on top of each potato, then fill with your favourite toppings – my Mexican beans (page 50) topped with shredded cheese are delicious with these potatoes!

*Look for potatoes that are considered good for baking, such as Sebagos (often labelled 'brushed' potatoes), Maris Piper, Desiree and King Edward.

+one pot wonder +dairy free (option) +vegan (option) +egg free +nut free +soy free +gluten free

Spicy lemongrass AND LENTIL SOUP

2 ½ cups (500 g) split red lentils, rinsed

½ cup (150 g) red curry paste*

6 cups (1.5 L) water

400 g can coconut cream

2 chicken-style stock cubes or 1 tablespoon faux-chicken stock powder (page 184)

2 lemongrass stalks, gently bashed with a rolling pin

4 fresh kaffir lime leaves

2 limes, juiced

¼ cup (60 ml) tamari

Serves 6
Hands-on time: 10 mins
Total slow cooker time: 4 or 8 hours

The lemongrass really shines in this soup, only possible thanks to the low and slow cooking, extracting every last bit of flavour! The red lentils offer great body, while the curry paste packs a punch. The lime juice added at the end freshens the whole dish up, while the tamari offers umami saltiness. It's an incredibly flavoursome and well-balanced dish, especially given the relatively short ingredient list! This recipe is one of my favourites for filling up the freezer – make it when you've got a bit of time so later you can enjoy delicious homemade meals at a moment's notice.

FIRST

1. Place red lentils, curry paste, water, coconut cream, stock cubes or stock powder, lemongrass and kaffir lime leaves in slow cooker. Stir to combine. Cover and cook for 4 hours on high or 8 hours on low.

4 OR 8 HOURS LATER

2. Remove lemongrass stalks and lime leaves. Add lime juice and tamari.

3. Puree using a stick blender, food processor or blender until smooth (if using a blender or food processor you will need to do this in batches).

Ladle into serving bowls or keep warm in the slow cooker until ready to serve. Delicious drizzled with my chilli and fennel seed infused oil (page 181).

For a vegan and vegetarian option, ensure your curry paste isn't made with shrimp. Homemade curry paste packs a lot more flavour and punch than commercial varieties, so if you've made your own (go you!) reduce the quantity by about a quarter.

fresh and light

+freezer friendly +one pot wonder +dairy free +vegan +egg free +nut free +soy free (option) +gluten free

77

This chapter contains the rich stews, soups and curries you expect when you think about slow cookers, but also a whole host of new and tasty options like crispy-fried mac 'n' cheese (vegan version included!), satay laksa, noodles, pasta – all cooked in the slow cooker! Most recipes take 4–5 hours on high or 5–10 hours on low. I use the low, long cooking options for days when I'm at work, putting the slow cooker on before I leave in the morning to have dinner ready when I return, or for overnight cooking of delicious meals ready to decant into food flasks for lunch or to load into containers for the freezer. The high setting I find handy for putting something on in the morning for a hot lunch, or on weekends when I might head to the market in the morning, returning early afternoon with enough time to get the fresh produce into the slow cooker for dinner.

hearty
and
comforting

THICK AND SAUCY *veg* BOLOGNESE

2 tablespoons extra virgin olive oil

2 brown onions, thinly sliced

3 garlic cloves, diced

2 carrots, finely diced

2 celery sticks, finely diced

1 eggplant, diced

400 g swiss brown mushrooms, diced

200 g pitted kalamata olives, diced

500 g ripe tomatoes, diced

¼ cup (70 g) red miso paste*

2 tablespoons maple syrup

2 chicken-style stock cubes or 1 tablespoon faux-chicken stock powder (page 184)

3 teaspoons ground sweet paprika

700 g passata (page 167)

1 potato, peeled and grated

Serves 6
Hands-on time: 15 mins
Total slow cooker time:
4 ½ or 8 ½ hours

This sauce is such a favourite of mine because it's rich, hearty and satisfying, while also being a big dose of veggies! And it couldn't be further from a watery sauce – in fact it's so thick and luscious we had to water it down to make lasagne. Make this recipe throughout spring, summer and autumn when these veggies are plentiful, cheap and at their best, loading up the freezer to get you through winter or whenever you need a quick meal. Heat up a container, cook some pasta and you've got the ultimate bowl food, faster than you could order Uber Eats.

FIRST

1. Heat oil in a large frypan over medium heat. Once hot, add onion and sauté for 5-10 minutes or until soft. Add garlic and continue cooking for a couple of minutes. Transfer to slow cooker.

2. In this order, add carrot, celery, eggplant, mushrooms, olives, tomatoes, miso paste, maple syrup, stock cubes or stock powder, paprika and passata to slow cooker. Cover and cook for 4 hours on high or 8 hours on low.

4 OR 8 HOURS LATER

3. Add grated potato, fold through, incorporating well. Cover and cook for a further 30 minutes on high.

And your bolognese is ready to serve! My favourite option is to ladle the sauce over penne or rigatoni and garnish with a sprinkling of cheese and fresh greens (pictured). This sauce is also great as a shepherd's pie base, a pie filling, pasta bake sauce, served over creamy polenta, stuffed in capsicums or inside a jacket potato (see page 76 for my slow cooker jacket potato recipe).

If avoiding gluten and soy, ensure miso paste is gluten and soy free – soy-free miso is hard to find but it can be done!

hearty and comforting

+freezer friendly +dairy free +vegan +egg free +nut free +soy free +gluten free

Creamy potato
AND PEA
MASSAMAN

- 1 tablespoon extra virgin olive oil
- 1 brown onion, diced
- 5 garlic cloves, diced
- 4 cm knob ginger, finely grated
- ¾ cup (225 g) massaman curry paste*
- 1.5 kg baby potatoes, quartered
- ¾ cup (210 g) smooth peanut butter
- 3 chicken-style stock cubes or 1 ½ tablespoons faux-chicken stock powder (page 184)
- 2 × 400 ml cans coconut cream
- 2 medium Desiree potatoes, peeled and grated
- 5 stalks silverbeet, stalks and leaves thinly sliced
- 2 cups (240 g) frozen peas
- 1 tablespoon fine salt

Serves 8
Hands-on time: 20 mins
Total slow cooker time:
4 or 7 hours

This recipe has to be one of the thickest curries going round, an ode to those who think slow cooked food is watery! I love my curries rich and creamy – the thicker the better. In this case I've used coconut cream, grated potato and a big dollop of peanut butter in the sauce, which really takes the richness to the next level. No one will feel like they're missing out with this vegan recipe! It's a great one to make when entertaining, no matter the eating preferences of your guests.

FIRST

1. Heat oil in a large frypan over medium heat. Once hot, add onion and sauté for 5–10 minutes or until soft. Add garlic and ginger, continue cooking for a couple of minutes. Add curry paste, sauté for 2 minutes.

2. In this order, place baby potatoes, sautéed onion mixture, peanut butter, stock cube or stock power and coconut cream in slow cooker. Cover and cook for 3 hours on high or 6 hours on low.

3 OR 6 HOURS LATER

3. Add grated potato, silverbeet, peas and salt. Fold everything through, giving it a good stir and making sure you transfer the potatoes from the bottom of the slow cooker to the top. Cover and cook for a further 1 hour on high.

Massaman curry is done! Serve with some combination of roasted peanuts, fresh coriander, fried shallots, sliced chilli, roti bread and fluffy rice.

*The best curry pastes are always homemade, but if purchasing and you want to keep this recipe vegetarian and vegan, look for a thick paste made without shrimp. If you've got red curry paste on hand you can use that instead of the massaman paste.

+freezer friendly +dairy free +vegan +egg free +soy free +gluten free

GARLICKY *split pea* DAHL

- 2 cups (400 g) yellow split peas, rinsed
- 2 chicken-style stock cubes or 1 tablespoon faux-chicken stock powder (page 184)
- 4 cm knob ginger, finely grated
- 1 tablespoon curry powder
- 1 tablespoon ground turmeric
- 1 teaspoon chilli flakes
- 4 cups (1 L) water
- ¼ cup (60 g) butter*
- ¼ cup (60 ml) extra virgin olive oil
- 2 brown onions, thinly sliced
- 6 garlic cloves, diced
- 1 teaspoon cumin seeds
- 100 g baby spinach leaves

Serves 6
Hands-on time: 15 mins
Total slow cooker time:
4 ½ or 9 hours

This recipe is delicious, yet deceptively simple. The fried onion, garlic and cumin seeds add a flavoursome sumptuousness, while the slow cooked split peas are soft and satisfying. It's like a curry, but with less spice and more richness. I love this for an easy meal with some fluffy white rice, but it also makes a great addition to an Indian banquet alongside a veggie curry, rice, roti, roasted cauliflower, mango chutney and all the trimmings. Even better the day after it's made.

FIRST

1. In this order, place split peas, stock cubes or powder, ginger, curry powder, turmeric, chilli and water in slow cooker. Cover and cook for 4 ½ hours on high or 9 hours on low.

4 ½ OR 9 HOURS LATER

2. Heat butter and oil in a large frypan over medium heat. Add onion, sauté for 10 minutes or until soft. Add garlic and cumin seeds and continue cooking until garlic is golden and cumin fragrant. Add mixture to slow cooker along with spinach leaves. Fold through until well combined and spinach has wilted.

Serve with rice, flatbreads, roti, naan, a dollop of coconut yoghurt (page 171), fresh coriander, lemon wedges, pickled red onion, raita (page 192), apple and mint chutney (page 193) or chilli flakes.

Use a plant-based butter for a dairy-free and vegan option.

hearty and comforting

+freezer friendly +dairy free (option) +vegan (option) +egg free +nut free +soy free +gluten free

MAC 'N' CHEEEEZE

2 cups (300 g) raw cashews

1 chicken-style stock cube or 2 teaspoons faux-chicken stock powder (page 184)

2 tablespoons white miso paste

2 tablespoons extra virgin olive oil

2 garlic cloves, peeled

3 teaspoons fine salt

4 cups (1 L) water

2 cups (500 ml) soy milk

½ cup (30 g) nutritional yeast flakes*

500g dried macaroni pasta

Serves 5
Hands-on time: 10 mins
Total slow cooker time:
3 hours or 5 ½ hours

Cheeeeze you say? This recipe doesn't actually contain any cheese or dairy at all – it's a super creamy, vegan, faux mac 'n' cheese! And I tell you what, given my dad (who claims to be allergic to vegan food) enjoyed two bowls of this, we are onto a winner. It's also a super easy recipe, with everything including the pasta cooked in the slow cooker bowl. Served straight away it's luscious and creamy, but my favourite trick is to pop it in the fridge right after cooking and then the next day fry it up in olive oil on the stove – not only do you get that cheesy pasta, you also get golden-fried crunchy bits. If dairy is off the menu for you, I may just be your new best friend.

FIRST

1. Place cashews, stock cube or stock powder, miso paste, oil, garlic, salt, water, soy milk and nutritional yeast flakes in slow cooker. Stir to combine. Cover and cook for 2 ½ hours on high or 5 hours on low.

2 ½ OR 5 HOURS LATER

2. Puree on high using a stick blender, food processor or high-powered blender until smooth. Keep going for longer than you think – you don't want your sauce grainy!

3. Add pasta and give it a good stir, ensuring pasta is fully submerged. Cover and cook for 30 minutes on high (no longer or you risk the pasta being overcooked).

4. Give it another good stir – you're going to be scared the recipe hasn't worked but just keep stirring! Test your pasta – it should be cooked al dente, but if not, cover and cook for a further 10 minutes on high.

+one pot wonder +dairy free +vegan +egg free

Best served straight away or refrigerated for frying later – don't leave in the slow cooker or your pasta will continue to cook. For full instructions on frying your mac 'n' cheese, follow steps 4 and 5 on page 92).

*Nutritional yeast flakes is a dairy-free and vegan ingredient that does an impressive impersonation of cheese, especially when blended with creamy ingredients like soy milk and cashew nuts. It's a flaky yellow powder available from health food stores and some supermarkets.

Tip: I consider the above the base recipe, and you can add your own flourishes as desired. I like adding in ½ teaspoon chilli flakes, 1 teaspoon sweet paprika or 1 teaspoon ground cumin at step 1.

SATAY LAKSA

1 tablespoon extra virgin
    olive oil

1 brown onion, diced

4 garlic cloves, diced

2 tablespoons curry
    paste*

1 cup (280 g) peanut
    butter

8 cups (2 L) water

400 ml can coconut
    cream

2 tablespoons tamari**

4 chicken-style
    stock cubes or
    2 tablespoons faux-
    chicken stock powder
    (page 184)

300 g dried udon
    noodles or spaghetti

1 cup (120 g) frozen peas

200 g button
    mushrooms, thinly
    sliced

2 heads bok choy, leaves
    separated and halved
    lengthways

2 limes, juiced

Serves 6
Hands-on time: 20 mins
Total slow cooker time:
2 ½ or 4 ½ hours

Not entirely sure if satay laksa is a thing, but I'm making it one! Spicy and warming coconut broth with a hearty dose of peanut butter, giving a rich and flavoursome satay feel. We've then got udon noodles that we're cooking in the slow cooker along with everything else, allowing the noodles to soak up all the delicious flavours and meaning we've got one less pot to worry about and wash up – double win! This is one seriously delicious dinner.

FIRST

1. Heat oil in a large frypan over medium heat. Once hot, add onion and sauté for 5–10 minutes or until soft. Add garlic and curry paste, continue cooking for a couple of minutes. Transfer to slow cooker.

2. Add peanut butter, water, coconut cream, tamari and stock cubes or stock powder, stir well to combine. Cover and cook for 2 hours on high or 4 hours on low.

2 OR 4 HOURS LATER

3. Give everything a good stir, scraping the bottom of the slow cooker and making sure peanut butter is mixed through. Add noodles or spaghetti, peas and mushrooms. Ensure noodles or spaghetti are fully submerged. Cover and cook for 30 minutes on high (no longer or you risk noodles being overcooked).

4. Add bok choy and lime juice and give everything a good stir. Test if noodles are cooked. If so, serve up! If not, cover and cook for a further 10 minutes on high.

Ladle into bowls, ensuring a good mix of broth, noodles and veggies. Serve with some combination of fresh coriander, roasted peanuts, thinly sliced spring onions, fried shallots and toasted sesame seeds.

Use whatever type of south-east Asian curry paste you prefer or have on hand (I usually use Thai red). To keep this recipe vegetarian and vegan, make your own or, if purchasing, look for a thick paste made without shrimp.

**Tamari is similar to soy sauce although it has a stronger, more complex flavour. It is my pick for Asian dishes, but you can use soy sauce instead. Available from Asian grocers and health food stores. For a soy-free option, use coconut aminos.*

hearty and comforting

+dairy free +vegan +egg free +soy free (option)

Thick and chunky
MINESTRONE SOUP

¼ cup (60 ml) extra virgin olive oil

1 brown onion, diced

3 garlic cloves, diced

2 potatoes, peeled and cut into 1 cm cubes

2 carrots, diced

2 celery sticks, diced

1 kg ripe tomatoes, diced

4 chicken-style stock cubes or 2 tablespoons faux-chicken stock powder (page 184)

2 sprigs rosemary

2 bay leaves

1–2 red chillies, diced

3 teaspoons fine salt

700 g passata*

4 cups (1 L) water**

400 g can four bean mix, rinsed and drained

½ bunch silverbeet, stalks and leaves finely chopped

350g dried macaroni

In fact, my minestrone is so thick and chunky it's been described as a stew . . . but that's just because I want all the delicious ingredients in there – the root veggies, the greens, the beans, the pasta . . . the lot! This is one soup not lacking oomph. You can always decrease the veggies to only 1 potato, carrot and celery stick if you like your soup thinner, or you could skip the pasta or beans. It makes a substantial amount, which is all part of the plan as this soup really does taste better when it's had a chance to sit for a day or more, either in the fridge or freezer, so it's a great one for leftovers. Heat up on the stove, ladle into a food flask and you've got the most perfect lunch on a chilly day.

FIRST

1. Heat oil in a large frypan over medium heat. Once hot, add onion and sauté for 5–10 minutes or until soft. Add garlic and continue cooking for a couple of minutes.

2. Place potatoes in slow cooker, spreading evenly across the bottom. Layer on top first carrot, then celery. Then, in this order, add tomatoes, stock cubes or stock powder, rosemary, bay leaves, chilli, salt, passata and water. Do not stir. Cover and cook for 4 hours on high, or 8 hours on low.

4 OR 8 HOURS LATER

3. Give everything a really good stir, then add beans, silverbeet and macaroni, pushing down with the back of a spatula if necessary, ensuring that it is fully submerged. Cover and cook for 30 minutes on high (no longer or you risk overcooking the pasta).

4. Give it another good stir and test your pasta – it should be cooked al dente, but if not, cover and cook for a further 10 minutes on high.

+freezer friendly +dairy free +vegan +egg free +nut free +soy free

Serves 8
Hands-on time: 20 mins
Total slow cooker time:
4 ½ or 8 ½ hours

Ladle into big soup bowls and garnish with some grated cheese or fresh parsley, if you like, and serve with a thick slice of good-quality bread.

*See page 167 to make your own!

**Measure out your water and then tip some into the empty passata jar – give it a good shake and then add to your slow cooker. This means we get every last drop of that tomatoey goodness and our jars are easy to clean, ready for the next batch of homemade passata.

fresh yoghurt raita
(page 192)
and lively apple and
mint chutney (page 193)

EASY INDIAN
chana masala

1 tablespoon extra virgin olive oil

2 brown onions, thinly sliced

6 garlic cloves, diced

4 cm knob ginger, finely grated

3 cups (600 g) dried chickpeas, rinsed*

500 g ripe tomatoes, diced finely**

400 g can coconut cream

⅓ cup (40 g) curry powder

1 chicken-style stock cube or 2 teaspoons faux-chicken stock powder (page 184)

2 teaspoons fine salt

4 cups (1 L) water

½ cup (65 g) ground cashews***

Serves 8
Hands-on time: 15 mins
Total slow cooker time: 6 or 12 hours + 10 mins standing

This would be one of my favourite Indian curries – tender chickpeas in a rich and flavoursome gravy. It tastes amazing straight out of the slow cooker, and only gets better and better over the coming days, as curries tend to! I often make this one when entertaining as you can really make a banquet out of it – serve with roti, rice, pilaf, raita (page 192), mango chutney, fresh apple and mint chutney (page 193), roasted cauliflower . . . so many delicious options. I also love how easy it is to use dried chickpeas in this recipe rather than canned – they have so much more flavour and bitey texture, and it's a much better option for our health and the environment.

FIRST

1. Heat oil in a large frypan over medium heat. Once hot, add onion and sauté for 5–10 minutes or until soft. Add garlic and ginger, continue cooking for a couple of minutes.

2. In this order, place chickpeas, tomatoes, onion mixture, coconut cream, curry powder, stock cube or powder, salt and water in slow cooker. Cover and cook for 6 hours on high or 12 hours on low.

6 OR 12 HOURS LATER

3. Add ground cashews and give everything a really good stir. Allow to stand, covered, for 10 minutes to thicken.

Serve whenever ready – this curry will happily sit for hours on the keep warm function or can be easily reheated on the stove another day.

*The older the chickpeas, the longer they take to cook. If yours have been in the pantry for years, I'd recommend soaking them in boiling water for an hour or two before adding to the slow cooker, or factor in an extra 30 minutes or so in the slow cooker.

**Fresh tomatoes are always my pick, but you can use a 400 g can of diced tomatoes for this recipe.

***Ground cashews are simply raw cashews ground down to a fine powder. Sometimes called cashew flour or meal, you can buy it from supermarkets and health food stores, but it's much better if you can mill it fresh yourself using a high-powered blender, food processor or coffee grinder.

+freezer friendly +dairy free +vegan +egg free +soy free +gluten free

CRISPY FRIED
mac 'n' cheese

700 g dried macaroni pasta

¼ cup (60 ml) extra virgin olive oil + 1 tablespoon extra

4 cups (1 L) full-fat milk

1 cup (250 ml) water

2 teaspoons Dijon mustard

2 teaspoons sweet paprika

3 teaspoons fine salt

2 chicken-style stock cubes or 1 tablespoon faux-chicken stock powder (page 184)

2 sprigs fresh thyme (optional)

250 g grated cheese*

Serves 6
Hands-on time: 20 mins
Total slow cooker time:
1 ½ hours + 2 hours chilling

I said hearty and comforting, and it doesn't get any more indulgent than fried mac 'n' cheese! You're going to have to trust me with this one as it all sounds a little crazy – cooking the pasta for 1.5 hours and you're still not allowed to eat it (what?!). But I promise you it works, with the result being a rich and oozy macaroni and cheese with a golden, crispy-fried cheese crust. Like a great toasted sandwich, only better. After a long day, at work (or a big night out!) you'll be so happy you've got this baby in the fridge, ready to hit the frypan and serve within 10 minutes. Plonk in a bowl, sit yourself on the couch and enjoy.

FIRST

1. Place pasta, ¼ cup oil, milk, water, mustard, paprika, salt, stock cubes or powder and thyme (if using) in slow cooker. Give everything a good stir, and ensure all pasta is submerged. Cover and cook for 1 hour on high (no longer or you risk overcooking the pasta).

1 HOUR LATER

2. Add cheese and give everything a good stir, folding the pasta from the bottom of the slow cooker up to the top. It's not going to look pretty at this stage but hang in there. If you can see the thyme sprigs (if using), pull them out. Make sure all pasta is submerged, then cover and cook for a further 30 minutes on high (again, timing is important here).

3. Give it another good stir and test your pasta – it should be cooked al dente, but if not, cover and cook for a further 10 minutes on high.

4. Once your pasta is cooked, remove from slow cooker immediately and transfer to a glass or plastic container. Cool slightly, then refrigerate for minimum 2 hours.

+egg free +nut free +soy free

5. When ready to serve, heat remaining 1 tablespoon olive oil in a large frypan over medium-high heat. Once hot, add in your cold pasta and allow to cook for 3 minutes or until a golden crust forms. Fold over to redistribute and wait another 3 minutes until crust forms. Do this a couple more times until you have a nice combination of oozy creamy pasta and golden crispy fried cheese.

Serve immediately nice and hot. I am quite partial to adding a sprinkling of chilli flakes or sriracha hot chilli sauce.

*You can use any combination of grated cheese you like -- I usually use a mix of cheddar, tasty and mozzarella, but you can also use parmesan, gouda, fontina, gruyere or pepper jack.

Smoky MOROCCAN STEW

1 cup (200 g) dried
  chickpeas, rinsed

1 cup (200 g) split red
  lentils, rinsed

500 g pumpkin, peeled
  and roughly chopped

1 kg ripe tomatoes,
  roughly chopped

700 g passata*

2 garlic cloves, diced

2 chicken-style stock
  cubes or 1 tablespoon
  faux-chicken stock
  powder (page 184)

¼ cup (60 ml) extra virgin
  olive oil

¼ cup (60 ml) red wine
  vinegar

¼ cup (75 g) harissa
  paste**

2 tablespoons sweet
  paprika

2 tablespoons smoked
  paprika

1 tablespoon ground
  cumin

1½ cups (375 ml) water

3 teaspoons fine salt

One of my favourite tricks to get the super carnivores among us (like my dad) to enjoy a vegetarian or vegan meal is smoky flavours – I think it must remind them of a barbecue, and therefore meat! This stew is hearty thanks to the lentils, chickpeas and tomatoes, full of flavour thanks to the harissa and spices, and rich and smoky thanks to the passata, smoked paprika and liquid smoke. It's got the tick of approval many times around the dinner (and breakfast!) table.

FIRST

1. Place chickpeas in slow cooker, spreading evenly across the bottom. Layer on top lentils first, then pumpkin. Then, in this order, add tomatoes, passata, garlic, stock cube or stock powder, oil, vinegar, harissa paste, sweet paprika, smoked paprika, cumin and water. Do not stir. Cover and cook for 6 hours on high or 12 hours on low.

6 OR 12 HOURS LATER

2. Add salt and liquid smoke (if using). Give everything a really good stir, breaking up the pumpkin as you go – this will thicken the stew.

Serve with garlic bread, hot buttered sourdough, toasted cheese sandwiches, couscous or spinach salad, possibly topped with a dollop of yoghurt, a drizzle of pomegranate molasses and some julienned cucumber for freshness. This would also be delicious underneath two poached eggs for breakfast.

+freezer friendly +one pot wonder +dairy free +vegan +egg free +nut free +soy free +gluten free

1.5 teaspoons liquid
   smoke (optional)***

Serves 8
Hands-on time: 10 mins
Total slow cooker time:
6 or 12 hours

*See page 167 if you want to make your own.

**Harissa paste is a concentrated, fiery concoction made from blended peppers, oil and spices. While it is traditionally used in North African and Middle Eastern cooking, I find a small amount does great things for almost any cuisine (I always have a jar in the fridge!). I add a teaspoon or two to any dish that needs a flavour boost, including pasta sauces, ragus, curries, roast vegetables, tagines, soups, noodle dishes, couscous and risottos. You can even stir the paste through mayonnaise or Greek yoghurt to make a dipping sauce or dressing. Make your own or purchase from delis in jars or tubes.

***Liquid smoke is one of my favourite ingredients for creating big, complex, meaty flavours without the meat – or the work! It's literally smoke in water. A 250 ml bottle will last you forever as you only use a tiny bit at a time, and you always add it at the end of cooking to preserve the flavour. I also use it to make my facon (fake bacon)! Available online.

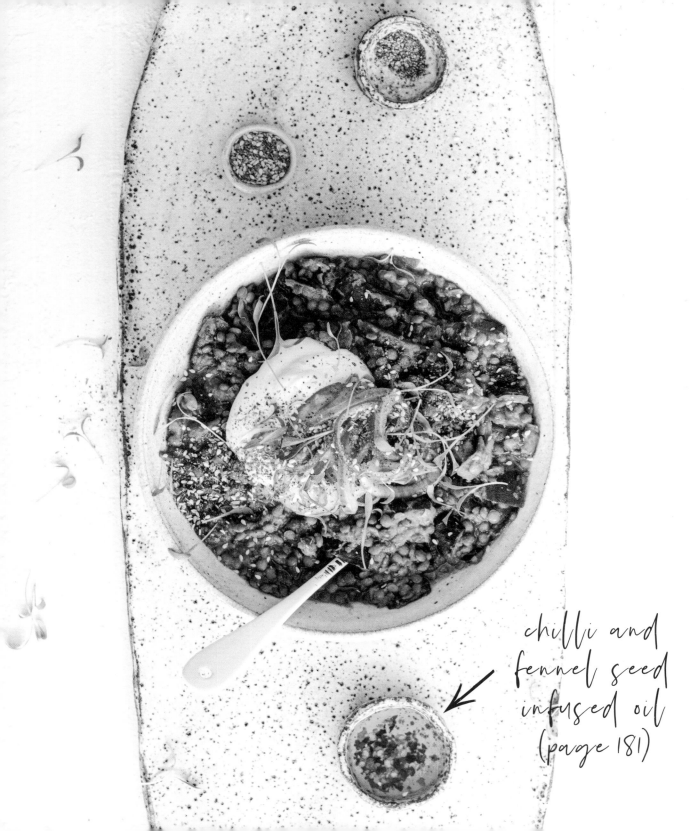

chilli and
fennel seed
infused oil
(page 181)

Middle Eastern
EGGPLANT
AND LENTILS

- 1 cup (200 g) French green lentils, rinsed
- 3 garlic cloves, diced
- 2 eggplants, ends trimmed, cut into 2 cm cubes
- 250 g cherry tomatoes, stems removed
- 1 chicken-style stock cube or 2 teaspoons faux-chicken stock powder (page 184)
- 1 teaspoon ground cumin seeds
- 1 teaspoon ground coriander seeds
- 1 cup (250 ml) water
- ½ cup (125 ml) white wine or extra water
- 2 tablespoons extra virgin olive oil
- 1 red onion, thinly sliced
- 3 teaspoons fine salt
- ¾ cup (180 ml) white vinegar
- Balsamic reduction or vincotto, to serve

Think of Ottolenghi's fresh and vibrant Middle Eastern flavour combinations when it comes to this recipe, for it was him that I was channelling! We've got delicious French lentils (yes, they really are a lot better than standard green lentils), perfectly cooked eggplant and juicy cherry tomatoes, topped with sweet balsamic reduction, properly pickled onions for freshness, crème fraîche for richness and za'atar for serious flavour. It sounds a little strange, but it's a winning combination. It's one of the easiest recipes to pull together, yet presents beautifully and has an impressive air – perfect when entertaining, especially when served with big slabs of Turkish bread and a rocket, pear and pomegranate salad. Usually I don't include my serving suggestions or toppings in the ingredients list, but with this recipe it really wouldn't be complete without them.

FIRST

1. In this order, place lentils, garlic, eggplant, tomatoes, stock cube or stock powder, cumin, coriander, water, wine (if using, or extra water) and olive oil in slow cooker. Cover and cook for 4 hours on high or 8 hours on low.

2. Meanwhile, place onion, 1 teaspoon salt and white vinegar in a small bowl and stir to combine. Try and submerge the onion as much as possible in the vinegar. Set aside to pickle.

4 OR 8 HOURS LATER

3. Add remaining 2 teaspoons salt to slow cooker and give everything a really good stir.

4. Drain onions, transferring vinegar to a jar and storing it in the fridge for up to 6 months – use it to pickle your onions next time!

Recipe continued over page >

+freezer friendly +one pot wonder +dairy free (option) +vegan (option) +egg free +nut free +soy free +gluten free

Crème fraîche or coconut
   yoghurt (page 171), to
   serve

Za'atar, to serve*

Serves 5
Hands-on time: 15 mins
Total slow cooker time:
4 or 8 hours

RECIPE CONTINUED

Serve immediately, or happily leave to cool and serve at room
temperature – it's just as good. Drizzle with balsamic reduction or
vincotto then top with crème fraîche or coconut yoghurt, followed by
your freshly pickled onions and finally generously sprinkle with za'atar.

*Za'atar is a blend of spices and sesame seeds that usually includes thyme and sumac.
Sprinkle over hummus, serve with bread and olive oil or use it to garnish Middle Eastern
soups and stews. It's super easy to make your own, or look for ready-made mixes in delis
and the spice aisle.*

Rich and Flavoursome
LASAGNA FILLING

2 tablespoons extra virgin olive oil

2 brown onions, thinly sliced

4 garlic cloves, diced

3 large eggplants, diced into 1 cm cubes

500 g ripe tomatoes, diced into 1 cm cubes

200 g pitted kalamata olives, diced

¼ cup (70 g) red miso paste*

2 tablespoons maple syrup

2 chicken-style stock cubes or 1 tablespoon faux-chicken stock powder (page 184)

1 teaspoon dried rosemary

1 teaspoon dried thyme

1 teaspoon dried oregano

700 g passata**

½ cup (125 ml) red wine

In many ways, lasagna was the impetus for me writing this book. My sister Loryn is the lasagna queen, and for our sister Ellen's birthday she made enough vegan lasagna to feed a small army! She was making batch after batch of sauce in the thermo cooker, literally taking all afternoon, when I said, 'You should have done one big batch in the slow cooker.' To which she replied, 'I would if there were any decent vegetarian slow cooker recipes!' And, as they say, the rest is history.

FIRST

1. Heat oil in a large frypan over medium heat. Once hot, add onion and sauté for 5–10 minutes or until soft. Add garlic and continue cooking for a couple of minutes.

2. In this order, place eggplant, tomato, onion mixture, olives, miso paste, maple syrup, stock cubes or stock powder, rosemary, thyme, oregano, passata and red wine in slow cooker. Cover and cook for 4 hours on high or 8 hours on low.

4 OR 8 HOURS LATER

3. Give everything a really good stir.

Your lasagna sauce is ready! See page 102 to put your ultimate vegan lasagna together, but this sauce can also be used for an eggplant parmigiana, pasta bake or vegetarian moussaka. It's a little too wet for a standard pasta sauce, which is what makes it perfect for cooking those lasagna sheets.

+freezer friendly +dairy free +vegan +egg free +nut free +soy free (option) +gluten free (option)

Serves 8
Hands-on time: 20 mins
Total slow cooker time:
4 or 8 hours

*If avoiding gluten and soy, ensure miso paste is gluten and soy free — it's hard to find but it can be done!

**See page 167 to make your own!

ULTIMATE *vegan* LASAGNA

2 cups (300 g) raw cashews

3 cups (750 ml) boiling water

1 chicken-style stock cube or 2 teaspoons faux-chicken stock powder (page 184)

2 tablespoons white miso paste

2 garlic cloves, peeled

2 teaspoons fine salt

1 tablespoon arrowroot powder*

1 ½ cups (375 ml) soy milk

1 tablespoon extra virgin olive oil

1 batch rich and flavoursome lasagna filling (page 100)

375 g instant lasagna sheets

Serves 8
Hands-on time: 30 mins
Total oven time: 45 mins
+ 10 mins standing

I know, I know – this recipe isn't strictly a slow cooker recipe. But we've cooked the filling in the slow cooker, and to deprive you of my sister Loryn's amazing vegan bechamel just seemed mean! So turn back to the previous page, get your filling cooking, and once that's done come back here ready to assemble. Of course, you could cook your filling days or weeks in advance (if you freeze it) and pull it all together an hour and a half before you're ready to serve, or make the whole lasagna a day or two before serving and simply reheat it in the oven. So many options! And trust me, no one's going to notice it contains no meat or dairy.

1. Preheat oven to 180°C.

2. To make the vegan bechamel sauce, place cashews in large heatproof bowl and cover with boiling water. Stand for a minimum 5 minutes.

3. Add stock cube or stock powder, miso, garlic, salt, arrowroot and soy milk. Puree using a stick blender, food processor or high-powered blender until smooth. Process a little longer than you think – you don't want your sauce grainy.

4. Transfer to a saucepan and cook on medium heat for 5–10 minutes until thickened, stirring often.

5. Use olive oil to grease the bottom of a baking dish that's about 40 × 35 × 10 cm. If you don't have one that big, you can always do two smaller ones. Cover base with a layer of lasagna sheets, breaking sheets if needed. Spread with a third of the lasagna filling, then a third of the bechamel sauce. Top with another layer of lasagna sheets, then half the remaining filling and bechamel sauce. For the final round, top with a third layer of lasagna sheets followed by the remaining lasagna filling and bechamel sauce.

+freezer friendly +dairy free +vegan +egg free

6. Cover with foil and bake for 30 minutes.

7. Remove foil, then bake for a further 15 minutes, or until lasagna sheets are cooked (test with a skewer).

8. Remove from oven and let stand for 10 minutes.

Slice up and serve! It only gets better with age, so treasure those leftovers. Reheat, covered with foil, at 180°C in the oven (if frozen, defrost first).

*Arrowroot powder, also known as arrowroot flour or arrowroot starch, is a white, powdery flour made from a dried root crop that's naturally gluten-free, grain-free, vegan, paleo-friendly and a great thickener. Available from health food shops and the baking aisle of supermarkets.

Spicy THAI
RED CURRY

2 tablespoons extra virgin olive oil

2 brown onions, diced

8 garlic cloves, diced

6 cm knob ginger, finely grated

½ cup (150 g) red curry paste*

2 cups (400 g) dried chickpeas, rinsed

1 kg pumpkin, peeled and roughly chopped into 4 cm pieces

2 tablespoons tomato paste

1 chicken-style stock cube or 2 teaspoons faux-chicken stock powder (page 184)

400 ml can coconut cream

2 cups (500 ml) water

100 g baby spinach leaves

Serves 6
Hands-on time: 20 mins
Total slow cooker time:
6 or 12 hours

Tender chickpeas, cooked to perfection from scratch (much better flavour and texture – I'm never buying canned again!) in a thick and spicy gravy. I love that the pumpkin breaks up, creating the creamy sauce, adding flavour, sweetness and a secret serve of veggies! It's the curry paste that gives the heat to this recipe, so if spicy is not your thing use a mild curry paste, or less of it. Easy!

FIRST

1. Heat oil in a large frypan over medium heat. Once hot, add onion and sauté for 5–10 minutes or until soft. Add garlic and ginger, continue cooking for a couple of minutes. Add curry paste, sauté for 2 minutes.

2. In this order, place chickpeas, pumpkin, sautéed onion mixture, tomato paste, stock cube or stock power, coconut cream and water in slow cooker. Cover and cook for 6 hours on high or 12 hours on low.

6 OR 12 HOURS LATER

3. Add spinach and give everything a really good stir, breaking up pumpkin, which will thicken the curry.

Serve with steamed rice, rice pilaf, roti bread or poppadoms. Delicious accompanied by a cucumber raita (page 192), which is even better if it's made with your very own coconut yoghurt (page 171)!

*The best curry pastes are always homemade, but if purchasing and you want to keep this recipe vegetarian and vegan, look for a thick paste made without shrimp.

+freezer friendly +dairy free +vegan +egg free +nut free +soy free +gluten free

Fast-food NACHOS

2 × 400 g cans black beans, rinsed and drained

2 cups (320 g) frozen corn kernels

1 red capsicum, diced

½ cup (140 g) tomato paste

2 tablespoons Mexican spice mix*

2 teaspoons fine salt

300 g tortilla chips

3 cups (360 g) shredded cheese**

Toppings (optional)

Tomato salsa, guacamole, sour cream, chilli sauce, pickled jalapeños, BBQ sauce (page 169), salsa verde (page 197)

Serves 6
Hands-on time: 15 mins
Total slow cooker time:
1 or 2 hours

These nachos are seriously satisfying – they're a definite crowd pleaser and pulled together with minimal fuss and ingredients. You'll never pay for expensive Mexican take-out again. They're about as fast as a slow-cooked recipe could ever be, taking just over an hour, so they're a great one to have stashed up your sleeve for last-minute meals, especially if feeding a crowd (even the carnivores fronted up for seconds!). If you've made a batch of my best BBQ sauce (page 169) – go you! – you're definitely going to want to serve it alongside these nachos . . . sounds like a weird combination, but I promise, it really works.

FIRST

1. Place black beans, corn, capsicum, tomato paste, spice mix and salt in slow cooker. Stir everything to combine. Cover and cook for 1 hour on high or 2 hours on low.

1 OR 2 HOURS LATER

2. Preheat grill to medium.

3. In a large casserole dish, spread out half the tortilla chips. Give black bean mixture in slow cooker a really good stir, then evenly spread half over tortilla chips. Top with half the shredded cheese. Repeat with remaining ingredients: another layer of tortilla chips, the remaining bean mixture and then the remaining cheese. Grill for 5 minutes or until cheese is melted and just starting to go golden in parts.

Serve hot straight out of the oven. The toppings are nice additions, but it happily stands alone as a meal.

Look for a Mexican spice mix without fillers and sugar, or better yet make your own (see page 185 for my recipe). The one I buy contains garlic, chilli, cumin, onion, sweet paprika, black pepper, salt, oregano and parsley – nothing else.

**Use whatever melty cheese you like – dairy or vegan. My pick is mozzarella, tasty, cheddar or Monterey Jack – or even better, a combination!*

hearty and comforting

+dairy free (option) +vegan (option) +egg free +nut free +soy free +gluten free

Saucy vodka PASTA

2 tablespoons extra virgin olive oil

1 brown onion, thinly sliced

4 garlic cloves, diced

1 kg ripe tomatoes, diced, or tinned diced tomatoes

2 chicken-style stock cubes or 1 tablespoon faux-chicken style stock powder (page 184)

3 teaspoons fine salt

2 cups (500 ml) water

500 g penne pasta

½ cup (120 g) double cream or plant-based butter

½ cup (125 ml) vodka

Serves 4
Hands-on time: 20 mins
Total slow cooker time:
4 hours 40 mins or
8 hours 40 mins

Now this is one recipe that's perfect for entertaining. It will have everyone talking – vodka pasta?! And we're not cooking off the alcohol, so it's even got a kick! (1 standard drink per person, for anyone driving.) The sauce is your typical Italian pink or rose sauce, rich and silky, and we're using my favourite hack: cooking the pasta right in with the sauce in the slow cooker! Not only does it cut down on washing up, but the starch released as the pasta cooks adds a subtle body to the sauce. By the time you sit down for dinner, the chopping board, knife and frypan have long ago been washed, the kitchen is clean and the stage is set for a relaxing evening.

FIRST

1. Heat oil in a large frypan over medium heat. Once hot, add onion and sauté for 5–10 minutes or until soft. Add garlic and continue cooking for a couple of minutes. Transfer to slow cooker.

2. Add tomatoes, stock cubes or stock powder, salt and water. Cover and cook for 4 hours on high or 8 hours on low.

4 OR 8 HOURS LATER

3. Give everything a really good stir. Add pasta, pushing down with the back of a spatula if necessary, ensuring that pasta is fully submerged. Cover and cook for 30 minutes on high (this is one of those times you need to be exact with time or you'll overcook the pasta).

4. Add cream and vodka and give the pasta another really good stir. Cover and cook for a further 10 minutes on high.

5. Test pasta for doneness – it should be cooked al dente, but if not, cover and cook for a further 10 minutes on high.

Serve your pasta straight away – don't leave in the slow cooker on the keep warm setting or you'll overcook it. Delicious as is, but my favourite way to serve it is piled high with fresh rocket and a generous drizzle of my chilli and fennel seed infused oil (page 181).

+dairy free (option) +vegan (option) +egg free +nut free +soy free

Two-minute 'CHICKEN' NOODLES

4 cups (1 L) water

5 teaspoons faux-chicken stock powder (page 184)

1 tablespoon white miso paste

2 cups (300 g) mixed frozen vegetables

600 g instant ramen or fresh Singapore noodles*

Serves 4
Hands-on time: 5 mins
Total slow cooker time:
1 hour 10 mins

. . . that contain no chicken, and definitely take longer than 2 minutes! But you get the idea, right? Curly noodles in a salty, faux-chicken broth with a few token veggies floating around for good measure. Now I'm not professing I think this a meal – it's more of a hearty snack – but if the kids (or you!) have a penchant for the old instant noodles, then this recipe is sure to satisfy – and all without MSG, palm oil, artificial flavours and maltodextrin! Homemade is always best.

FIRST

1. Place water, stock powder, miso and frozen vegetables in slow cooker. Cover and cook for 1 hour on high.

1 HOUR LATER

2. Add noodles, submerging in the liquid. Cover and cook for 10 minutes on high – the timing is important as we don't want to overcook the noodles!

3. Use a fork to separate the noodles if they've clumped together.

Ladle broth and noodles into mugs, bowls or food flasks to take to work or school. Enjoy.

Purchased instant noodles make this recipe really authentic to 'two-minute noodles', but for an even healthier version, boil up 300 g dried ramen or udon noodles and add these into the slow cooker at step 2 and serve up immediately (no need to cook for 10 minutes). In a pinch, you could even use spaghetti.

+one pot wonder +dairy free +vegan +egg free +nut free

Smoky PULLED 'PORK'

600 g jackfruit in water or brine, drained*

¼ cup (70 g) tomato paste

¼ cup (90 g) golden syrup

2 tablespoons Worcestershire sauce**

1 ½ tablespoons Mexican spice mix (page 185)

3 teaspoons fine salt

4 garlic cloves, diced

1 ¼ teaspoons liquid smoke***

Serves 4
Hands-on time: 10 mins
Total slow cooker time: 2 or 4 hours

It's very rare I try to imitate meat in a recipe, but this one just turned out so meaty it was impossible not to call it pulled 'pork'! In tacos with my BBQ sauce (page 169) and pineapple salsa (page 195), it's seriously impressive, fooling even the most dedicated carnivore. Test it out yourself! The meaty secret lies in two special ingredients: jackfruit and liquid smoke. After a few hours cooking, the jackfruit shreds to the stringy texture of pulled meat, while the liquid smoke makes it taste like it's been cooked low and slow over hot coals for days. The hardest part about this recipe is finding those two ingredients – the actual method couldn't be any simpler if you tried. If you're planning your Mexican banquet in advance, the easiest place to get those ingredients is online.

FIRST

1. Place jackfruit, tomato paste, golden syrup, Worcestershire sauce, Mexican spice mix, salt and garlic in slow cooker. Stir to combine. Cover and cook for 2 hours on high or 4 hours on low.

2 OR 4 HOURS LATER

2. Add liquid smoke, stir to combine. Use two forks to shred jackfruit as you would meat.

Your pulled 'pork' is ready! It looks pretty meaty, don't you think? Serve in tacos, burritos, toasted cheese sandwiches, spring rolls or sliders. Even better when served with my BBQ sauce (page 169), salsa verde (page 197), hot sauce (page 175), raita (page 192) or pineapple salsa (page 195).

You'll find jackfruit in cans or cryovac packages from health food stores or online. As it becomes more and more popular, I've also recently seen it popping up in supermarkets. Make sure it's in water or brine, not syrup.

+freezer friendly +one pot wonder +dairy free +vegan +egg free +nut free +soy free +gluten free

**For this recipe to be vegetarian and vegan, look for an anchovy-free Worcestershire sauce, or better yet, make your own!

***Liquid smoke is essential for this recipe – find it in specialist food stores or online. A 250 ml bottle will last you a lifetime because a little goes a long way! My favourite is hickory-flavoured liquid smoke.

Note: This is a great recipe when entertaining a lot of people – set up a DIY taco station with this pulled 'pork' as the base and plenty of fresh and flavoursome toppings. You can make up to four times this recipe in a large slow cooker – scale up the ingredients accordingly and follow exactly the same method and cooking time.

HOSTING *a stress-free* MEXICAN FIESTA

THE FEAST

2 × Smoky pulled 'pork' (page 110)

Jazzy Mexican corn salad (page 118)

The best BBQ sauce (page 169)

No-joke hot sauce (page 175)

Punchy pineapple salsa (page 195)

Salsa verde (page 197)

+ guacamole (make your own!)

+ sour cream (buy)

+ grated cheese (buy)

+ corn tortillas or corn tacos (buy)

+ corn chips (buy)

+ lime wedges (buy)

Given the choice, I'd much rather eat at home, surrounded by friends and family, than at a fancy restaurant. Despite having to do the dishes, I always find these nights to be the most fun and authentic. I love the way good food brings people together, and this is never more true than with celebrations at home. Armed with a slow cooker and a little planning, entertaining really can be easy! One of my favourite things to cook for a crowd is a Mexican feast – so many of the components can be made in advance and it caters for almost all eating preferences. Individually, the recipes are accessible and achievable, but put together they create a spectacular meal. Here I've done all the planning for you, so now all you have to do is invite the guests and get cooking!

This menu is for a feast for eight. Cook all the recipes or just a couple – this is simply a guide to help with planning and preparation. The whole menu is vegan, dairy free, soy free, gluten free and nut free, providing you leave out the sour cream and opt for a vegan cheese (but then watch the soy!). So, no matter who your guests are, everyone will be catered for without having to prepare any special dishes. Lay out everything in the middle of the table banquet style and let people serve themselves – not only does this make it easier on the host (you!), it also builds a sense of community around the table. Lay most components out in advance, skip the nibbles and get straight into the main event once everyone arrives – that way you can sit down and relax with your guests straight away. Mission accomplished.

. . . and if it's autumn, I'd put on a batch of celebration quince syrup (page 159) to enjoy with a glass of sparkling wine on arrival. For summer I'd make a refreshing cocktail using my fiery ginger cordial (page 163). For spring I'd go for a batch of my modern mulled wine (page 153) and for winter my pick would be my sweet and spiced apple cider toddy (page 151) to enjoy after dinner.

THE WEEK BEFORE

1. Make a batch of BBQ sauce. Store in jars in the fridge.

2. Make a batch of hot sauce. Store in jars in the fridge.

1-2 DAYS BEFORE

1. Cook jazzy Mexican corn salad. If using coriander, don't mix it through yet. Store in a sealed container in the fridge.

2. Make a batch of pineapple salsa. Store in a sealed container in the fridge.

3. Make a batch of salsa verde. Store in a jar in the fridge.

DAY OF THE FEAST

1. Cook a double batch of the smoky pulled 'pork' – follow the same method and timing as in the recipe, just use double the ingredients. Keep in the slow cooker on the keep warm setting until ready to serve.

1 HOUR BEFORE GUESTS ARRIVE

1. Remove corn salad from the fridge and allow to come to room temperature. If using coriander, stir through now. Get it on the table.

2. Decant the BBQ sauce, hot sauce and salsa verde into cute ramekins and get them on the table.

3. Give the pineapple salsa a good stir, transfer to a pretty bowl and get it on the table.

4. Make a batch of guacamole – use plenty of lime juice to prevent the avocado browning. Get it on the table.

5. Preheat oven to a moderate heat, then warm tacos and corn chips.

6. Place sour cream, cheese and lime wedges on the table.

TO SERVE

1. Take the pulled 'pork' to the table in the slow cooker insert (use pot holders and a heat-proof placemat).

2. Place warm tacos and corn chips on table.

Sit down, relax and enjoy the delicious food and the company of your guests. After all, that is the point!

punchy pineapple salsa (page 195)

cheat's
salsa verde
(page 197)

no-joke hot sauce
(page 175)

There is another part of your meals the slow cooker can help with! Here we've got tasty sides to accompany whatever else you're cooking and starters to whet the appetite (check out my polenta chips, page 122!). But the options don't end there – use my classic mashed potato (page 125) to top your pie, or bulk out my zesty pearl barley salad (page 120) with roast veggies for a satisfying meal. The opportunities are endless! And it's all easy.

super sides

Jazzy Mexican
CORN SALAD

4 fresh corncobs, kernels only

400 g can black beans, rinsed and drained

1 chicken-style stock cube or 2 tsp faux-chicken stock powder (page 184)

2 teaspoons smoked paprika

2 tablespoons extra virgin olive oil

1 red onion, finely diced

1 lime, juiced

1 teaspoon fine salt

½ cup (150 g) mayonnaise*

2 spring onions, finely chopped

Handful fresh coriander, finely chopped (optional)**

Serves 6
Hands-on time: 15 mins
Total slow cooker time: 2 or 4 hours

Fresh corn, lightly cooked with black beans and smoked paprika, tossed with lime-pickled red onion, creamy mayonnaise and spring onions. It's a pretty jazzy salad! Great served as a side dish but also doubles as a brilliant filling in burritos. It also keeps really well in the fridge, unlike most salads, so it's perfect to make on the weekend and then pull out for all manner of lunches and dinners throughout the week. Head to your local produce market and pick up the freshest ears of corn you can find – the sooner corn is eaten after picking, the sweeter it will be (so if you grow your own you're in luck). Plant seeds (dried kernels!) in spring.

FIRST

1. Place corn kernels, black beans, stock cube or stock powder, smoked paprika and oil in slow cooker. Stir to combine. Cover and cook for 2 hours on high or 4 hours on low.

2. Meanwhile, combine red onion, lime juice and salt in a large mixing bowl. Set aside to marinate.

2 OR 4 HOURS LATER

3. Transfer slow cooker contents to mixing bowl containing onion. Add mayonnaise, spring onions and coriander (if using). Toss together and combine well, ensuring onion and lime juice are evenly dispersed.

Serve as part of any Mexican spread – tacos (page 55), nachos (page 105), burritos, you name it. Use to fill jacket potatoes (page 76) or bulk up with spinach and tomato for a fresh meal on its own. Serve immediately or happily refrigerate for up to 3 days.

*For this recipe to be vegan and egg free, you'll need an egg-free mayonnaise. I always make my own, but if you're going to purchase look for a high-quality brand – it makes all the difference.

**If you like the taste of coriander, definitely use it in this recipe! If you don't, leave it out – it will overpower your palate. It'll still taste great.

+one pot wonder +dairy free +vegan (option) +egg free (option) +nut free +soy free +gluten free

Toasty ROSEMARY POTATOES

2 tablespoons extra virgin olive oil

3 Desiree potatoes, cut into wedges*

1 teaspoon garlic powder

1 teaspoon dried rosemary

1 teaspoon fine salt

Serves 4
Hands-on time: 10 mins
Total slow cooker time:
4 or 8 hours

Salty, flavoursome, perfectly cooked wedges of potato hot and ready when you walk in the door . . . sounds rather good to me! I've gone with a classic garlic and rosemary combo here, but honestly, the world's your oyster. Try smoked paprika and cumin, a Mexican spice blend, thyme, sage, oregano, chilli flakes or even garam masala! It all depends on what you're serving them with. Enjoy!

FIRST

1. Place all ingredients in slow cooker and toss to combine – you want all the potatoes coated in oil. Lay potatoes wedges as flat as possible across the bottom of your slow cooker. Cover and cook for 4 hours on high or 8 hours on low.

4 OR 8 HOURS LATER

And your potatoes are ready to go! Serve alongside anything and everything. Any leftovers? Cut into smaller pieces and toss with mayo and spring onions for an impromptu potato salad.

The Desiree potato is my pick for this recipe – they're generally easy to find – but you can use any all-rounder potato.

+one pot wonder +dairy free +vegan +egg free +nut free +soy free +gluten free

Fresh and zesty
PEARL BARLEY SALAD

1½ cups (300 g) pearl barley, rinsed

6 cups (1.5 L) water

2 chicken-style stock cubes or 1 tablespoon faux-chicken stock powder (page 184)

2 red shallots, thinly sliced

½ teaspoon fine salt

1 lemon, zest finely grated, juiced

2 tablespoons apple cider vinegar

2 teaspoons whole cumin seeds

¼ cup (60 ml) extra virgin olive oil

2 tablespoons raw honey or maple syrup

1 pomegranate, arils removed*

2 Lebanese cucumbers, thinly sliced

1 Granny Smith apple, cored and cubed

This salad, in my opinion, is sheer perfection. When you write a cookbook, you end up eating the same dish time and time again – my family and I test the recipes over and over to ensure they work every single time, and no food is ever wasted around here! I can tell you, after serve after serve of this salad, I still think it's one of my favourites – hearty and filling thanks to the barley, zesty thanks to the lemon and pomegranate, fresh thanks to the apple and cucumber, all with hints of sweetness and pops of flavour thanks to the honey and toasted cumin seeds.

FIRST

1. Place barley, water and stock cubes or powder in slow cooker. Stir to combine. Cover and cook for 3 hours on high or 6 hours on low.

2. In a large mixing bowl place shallots, salt, lemon zest and juice and apple cider vinegar. Mix to combine. Set aside to marinate.

3 OR 6 HOURS LATER

3. Check barley is tender and cooked through. If not, cover and cook for a further 30 minutes on high. Once cooked, drain any excess water and set barley aside.

4. Heat a small frypan over medium heat. Add cumin seeds and toast until fragrant, about 5 minutes.

5. Add cumin seeds to shallot mixture, along with cooked barley, oil, honey or maple syrup, pomegranate arils, cucumber and apple. Toss until well combined.

+dairy free +vegan (option) +egg free +nut free +soy free

Serves 6
Hands-on time: 15 mins
Total slow cooker time:
3 or 6 hours

Enjoy straight away or refrigerate for up to 3 days. Delicious as is, but this salad lends itself to so many other wonderful vegetable combinations. Try adding in roasted beetroot or pumpkin if you're bulking this up to be a meal on its own, or fresh rocket, mint or spinach for some extra freshness. Top with a generous dollop of tzatziki, raita (page 192), Greek yoghurt, feta, grilled haloumi or toasted almonds or pine nuts. So versatile – what a champ!

*Removing the arils from a pomegranate isn't the best job – I'm yet to manage it without a spray of pomegranate juice going everywhere! There are a few ways to do it, but I find the easiest is to just break the pomegranate apart section by section, removing the precious red jewels into one bowl and the inedible white pith into the other.

Real-deal POLENTA CHIPS

9 cups (2.25 L) water

4 chicken-style
   stock cubes or
   2 tablespoons faux-
   chicken stock powder
   (page 184)

350g traditional polenta*

Extra virgin olive oil,
   to drizzle

Serves 10
Hands-on time: 15 mins
Total slow cooker time:
3 or 6 hours + 1 hour
chilling + 30 mins
baking

Soft and fluffy on the inside, golden and crispy on the outside, salty and flavoursome thanks to the stock. Just like the ones you love to order at the gastropub, except these will cost you next to nothing to make and they're baked in extra virgin olive oil instead of fried. This recipe makes a lot, which is great because they're so moreish everyone is going to eat more than their allocated serve. Alternatively, you can keep the unbaked (cooked) polenta in the fridge for up to 5 days and simply bake a few chips whenever you want them. Do the work once, enjoy throughout the entire week!

FIRST

1. Place water, stock cubes or powder and polenta in slow cooker, whisk to combine. Cover and cook for 3 hours on high or 6 hours on low.

3 OR 6 HOURS LATER

2. Using a pastry brush, grease a large casserole or baking dish (about 30 cm × 40 cm) liberally with olive oil.

3. Give polenta mixture a really good stir and pour into greased dish. Make sure to do this while your polenta is still piping hot as it will begin to set as it cools. Refrigerate mixture for a minimum 1 hour.

4. Preheat oven to 200°C.

5. Turn out polenta onto a large cutting board – it should easily fall from greased dish in one large slab. Cut into thick chips. Either grease or line two baking trays (use reusable silicone baking mats or baking paper, not foil). Place chips onto prepared trays, leaving a 1 cm gap between each chip. Brush with oil.

6. Bake for 30 minutes, or until lightly golden around the edges and starting to crisp.

+dairy free +vegan +egg free +nut free +soy free +gluten free

Polenta chips are ready! Try not to burn your mouth in your haste to enjoy one of these golden delights. Serve with herbed mayo, BBQ sauce (page 169), sweet chilli sauce or of course the classic, tomato sauce. I find these salty enough from the stock, but you might want to sprinkle with salt flakes.

*Make sure not to use instant polenta that has already been partially cooked — I find it never has as good a flavour or texture.

Classic POTATO MASH

2 kg potatoes, peeled and roughly chopped into 3 cm pieces*

2 garlic cloves, diced

2 cups (500 ml) water

2 chicken-style stock cubes or 1 tablespoon faux-chicken stock powder (page 184)

½ cup (125 g) butter, vegan butter or cream

1 cup (120 g) grated tasty cheese (optional)

Serves 8
Hands-on time: 10 mins
Total slow cooker time: 4 or 8 hours

Put this one on in the morning, give it a mash when you get home at night and Bob's your uncle. It doesn't really matter if the slow cooker clicks over to the keep warm setting for a couple of hours before mashing. You'd be hard-pressed to overcook the potatoes – it's a pretty forgiving recipe. Enjoy!

FIRST

1. Place potatoes, garlic, water and stock cubes or powder in slow cooker, submerging potatoes as much as possible. Cover and cook for 4 hours on high or 8 hours on low.

4 OR 8 HOURS LATER

2. Add butter or cream and cheese (if using), then mash using a potato masher until desired texture is achieved.

Serve immediately as is, use to top a pie, keep in the slow cooker on the keep warm setting to serve later, refrigerate for up to 3 days or freeze for longer!

Look for starchy potatoes that are good for mashing, such as Sebago (also known as 'brushed' potatoes), Yukon Gold and Russet. Failing that, Desiree (the ones with the pink skins) are readily available and do a fine job.

Tip: Too much mash? Not enough? Easy – double or halve the ingredients, then follow exactly the same method.

+freezer friendly +one pot wonder +dairy free (option) +vegan (option) +egg free +nut free +soy free +gluten free

LORYN'S
spiced lentil
SALAD

2 cups (400 g) French green lentils or black lentils, rinsed*

6 cups (1.5 L) water

1 bay leaf (optional)

1 lemon, zest finely grated, juiced

2 tablespoons apple cider vinegar

2 teaspoons fine salt

⅓ cup (80 ml) extra virgin olive oil

2 tablespoons Dijon mustard

1 tablespoon maple syrup

1 teaspoon ground cardamom

1 teaspoon ground cumin

½ teaspoon ground turmeric

½ teaspoon ground coriander

¼ teaspoon cayenne pepper

¼ teaspoon ground cloves

1 red onion, finely diced

½ cup (approximately 55g) currants

This recipe is the creation of my sister Loryn, and we all agree there's one thing she's better at than me in the kitchen – punchy, fresh salads. This one doesn't disappoint. A serious combination of spices that all marry together beautifully, especially combined with the sweetness of currants and the freshness of the cucumber and onion. In the words of YouTube sensation Nat's What I Reckon, 'Take it easy, Picasso – it's a bit like a Christmas tree, you can over-decorate it and it ends up falling over under the weight of your creativity.' That's how I feel about salads – they're deceptively difficult to get perfectly balanced, and more is not always better. But here, Loryn's got it just right.

FIRST

1. Place lentils, water and bay leaf (if using) in slow cooker. Cover and cook for 3 hours on high or 6 hours on low.

2. Meanwhile, place lemon zest and juice, vinegar, salt, oil, mustard, maple syrup, cardamom, cumin, turmeric, coriander, cayenne pepper and cloves in a jar and shake until well combined.

3. Place onion in a large mixing bowl and pour over dressing. Set aside.

3 OR 6 HOURS LATER

4. Check lentils are tender and cooked through. If not, cover and cook for a further 30 minutes on high. Once cooked, drain any excess water and rinse lentils with cold water. Discard bay leaf (if using).

5. Add cooked lentils, currants and cucumber to onion mixture, toss to combine, ensuring dressing and onion are evenly distributed.

+one pot wonder +dairy free +vegan +egg free +nut free +soy free +gluten free

1 Lebanese cucumber,
    diced

100 g rocket leaves

Serves 6
Hands-on time: 15 mins
Total slow cooker time:
3 or 6 hours + cooling

At this point, your salad is ready for serving, but will improve with a couple of hours in the fridge for all the flavours to marinate (or longer, as it really does get better with age). Preferably remove it from the fridge 30 minutes prior to serving to take the chill off, then toss with rocket. Like our fresh and zesty pearl barley salad (page 120), add roasted pumpkin or beetroot to bulk this up as a meal on its own, or top with a dollop of hummus (page 130), tzatziki, raita (page 192), Greek yoghurt, feta, grilled haloumi or toasted almonds or pine nuts. So many options, all delicious! It's a whole new recipe each time you serve it.

*French lentils are a type of green lentil, and a great pick for salads as they hold their shape when cooked. Available from supermarkets. Black lentils, also known as beluga lentils, are my favourite for this recipe, but they can be hard to get ... if you can find them, grab them!

SWEET POTATO *mash*

1.5 kg sweet potato, peeled and roughly chopped into 2 cm pieces

2 chicken-style stock cubes or 1 tablespoon faux-chicken stock powder (page 184)

1 garlic clove, diced (optional)

½ cup (125 ml) water

1 teaspoon fine salt

¼ cup (60 g) butter*

Serves 6
Hands-on time: 15 mins
Total slow cooker time: 3 ½ or 7 hours

For this recipe I love cooking the sweet potatoes in stock rather than plain water – it adds a decent whack of savoury flavour, which perfectly balances the natural sweetness of the (aptly named) sweet potato. It's a slightly softer texture than the starchier standard potato mash (page 125) but with more flavour and a nice dose of vitamin C. Try pairing it with a thick curry, like my easy Indian chana masala (page 91) for something a bit different.

FIRST

1. Place sweet potato, stock cubes or stock powder, garlic (if using), water and salt in slow cooker. Cover and cook for 3 ½ hours on high or 7 hours on low.

3 ½ OR 7 HOURS LATER

2. Add butter, wait a couple of minutes for it to melt. Mash with a potato masher until desired texture is achieved.

Serve immediately as is, use to top a pie, keep in the slow cooker on the keep warm setting to serve later, refrigerate for up to 3 days or freeze for longer! Puree any leftovers with a splash of thin cream and you've got a creamy pasta sauce. Serve tossed through fettuccine and topped with some crispy, fried sage leaves and toasted pine nuts. Yum!

Use a plant-based butter for a vegan and dairy-free option.

+freezer friendly +one pot wonder +dairy free (option) +vegan (option) +egg free +nut free +soy free +gluten free

Balsamic
BRUSSELS SPROUTS

1 kg brussels sprouts, ends trimmed, quartered

2 tablespoons extra virgin olive oil

3 teaspoons fine salt or salt flakes

1 cup (125 g) mixed nuts and seeds (a combination of sesame seeds, pumpkin seeds, sunflower seeds, pine nuts and slivered almonds)*

Balsamic reduction**

Serves 6
Hands-on time: 15 mins
Total slow cooker time:
2 or 4 hours

Brussels sprouts have a bad rap, but they're delicious! Especially when cooked the right way. The slow cooker cooks them through to tender perfection, with the a few charred bits around the edges – impressively reminiscent of the oven, without the effort. Topped with a sweet and sticky balsamic reduction and toasted nuts and seeds for flavour and crunch, this is an easy yet impressive side dish. Brussels sprouts are grown throughout summer but are ready to harvest in winter, so enjoy them in the cooler months when your other favourites are out of season.

FIRST

1. Place brussels sprouts (including any layers that have fallen off when you've trimmed the ends), oil and salt in slow cooker, stir to combine. Cover and cook for 2 hours on high or 4 hours on low.

2. Meanwhile, heat a large frypan over medium heat. Once hot, add nuts and seeds and stir continuously until golden. Don't leave the stove – they'll burn easily.

2 OR 4 HOURS LATER

To serve, transfer sprouts to a large serving bowl or platter, generously drizzle with balsamic reduction and top with toasted nuts and seeds. Voilà!

Use only seeds for a nut-free option.

**A balsamic reduction, also known as a balsamic glaze, is a thick and sweet dressing made from reducing down balsamic vinegar. Buy from good delicatessens or, better yet, make your own! Simmer balsamic vinegar in saucepan until reduced by half. I like to add in a little brown sugar and some orange juice.*

super sides

+dairy free +vegan +egg free +nut free (option) +soy free +gluten free

Rolls-Royce HUMMUS

1 cup (200 g) dried chickpeas, rinsed

2 garlic cloves, peeled

4 cups (1 L) water

1 lemon, juiced

¼ cup (70 g) hulled tahini*

⅓ cup (80 ml) extra virgin olive oil

1 ½ teaspoons fine salt

¾ teaspoon ground cumin

OPTIONAL TOPPING

¼ cup (60 ml) extra virgin olive oil

¼ cup (35 g) slivered almonds or pine nuts

½ teaspoon whole cumin seeds

2 dried figs, finely diced

1 tablespoon raw honey

Makes 3 cups

Hands-on time: 15 mins

Total slow cooker time: 5 or 10 hours

This may look like one of the longest recipes in this entire book . . . and for a dip! But I promise the hands-on part actually won't take that long at all, and this really will be the best hummus you've ever eaten. It'll make an impressive starter at your next pot-luck dinner or picnic, or accompaniment to a Middle Eastern feast or barbecue. The fig, nut and honey topping really is the icing on the cake here, but the hummus is still amazing without, so I've made it optional . . . and perhaps it's not necessary if you're spreading the hummus inside sandwiches or wraps. But, if you've got the ingredients, give it a go – it's pretty special.

FIRST

1. Place chickpeas, garlic and water in slow cooker. Cover and cook for 5 hours on high or 10 hours on low.

5 OR 10 HOURS LATER

2. Check chickpeas are tender. If not, continue cooking for 30 minutes on high.

3. Once cooked, drain chickpeas and garlic, reserving ½ cup of cooking liquid. Place chickpeas, garlic and ¼ cup cooking liquid in food processor or high-powered blender.

4. Add lemon juice, tahini, oil, salt and cumin, process for 1 minute. Using a spatula, scrape down sides and process for another 1 minute, until smooth, creamy and whipped. If hummus looks too thick or isn't becoming smooth, add remaining ¼ cup cooking liquid and continue processing. Transfer to pretty plate or bowl.

If you're making the topping:

5. Heat oil in a frypan over medium-low heat. Add nuts and cumin seeds and fry until lightly golden, moving frequently. Don't step away from the stove – it takes mere seconds for the nuts to go from golden to burnt. Turn off heat.

+dairy free +vegan (option) +egg free +nut free (option) +soy free +gluten free

6. Add figs and honey to frypan, stirring to combine and allowing the residual heat to warm them through. Pour mixture over hummus, ensuring you scrape all the sweet, flavoursome oil from the pan.

Best served immediately with fresh Turkish bread while hummus and toppings are still warm, but will happily keep in the fridge for up to 5 days.

Tahini is a paste made from ground toasted sesame seeds. I prefer the hulled version for my hummus, but if all you've got is unhulled, use that (it'll have a stronger, nuttier flavour). You can buy it in jars from supermarkets, delis and health food stores, or make your own.

I've got you covered, right through to dessert! And don't worry, there'll be enough time to cook it all. Some of these recipes need only an hour and a half in the slow cooker, perfect for putting on right before you sit down for dinner. Others need to be made at least 8 hours in advance and chilled, so you don't need to stress about timing – just get them on whenever you have the chance. For the puddings that fit into neither of these categories, give them the afternoon in the slow cooker and cook your main the day or night before and simply reheat – the soups, stews and curries will all taste better after resting.

sweet treats

SELF-
SAUCING
molten chocolate
PUDDING

1 cup (220 g) caster sugar

1 cup (150 g) plain flour*

¾ cup (75 g) cocoa powder

1 tablespoon instant
coffee (optional)

2 teaspoons baking powder

½ cup (125 ml) coconut milk

⅓ cup (80 ml) light-
flavoured extra virgin
olive oil, macadamia oil
or melted coconut oil

2 teaspoons vanilla extract

½ cup (110 g) brown sugar

1 ½ cups (375 ml) hot water

EXTRAS

2 L pudding basin or
small casserole dish
(preferably with lid) that
fits inside slow cooker

What could be better than a chocolate pudding, complete with molten chocolate sauce, where you only have a single pudding basin to wash up at the end?! Here we mix our batter in the same pudding basin we cook it in, meaning no slow cooker to clean and no mixing bowl or food processor to wash. It really is the laziest yet most satisfying dessert, perfect for any night of the week or special occasion.

FIRST

1. In pudding basin or casserole dish, place caster sugar, flour, ¼ cup (25 g) cocoa, coffee (if using), baking powder, coconut milk, oil and vanilla. Using a spatula, stir until well combined, then smooth down the top of the batter.

2. Sprinkle brown sugar and remaining ½ cup (50 g) cocoa over the top of the batter, then pour over hot water. It's important *not* to stir at this point! Cover pudding with lid or foil, sealing tightly.

3. Place inside slow cooker, then add water until pudding basin is two-thirds submerged. Cover and cook for 3 ½ hours on high.

+one pot wonder +dairy free +vegan +egg free +nut free (option) +soy free +gluten free (option)

Serves 6
Hands-on time: 10 mins
Total slow cooker time:
3 ½ hours + 10 mins
standing

3 ½ HOURS LATER

4. Remove pudding basin from slow cooker and allow to stand for 10 minutes.

Chocolate pudding is ready! Spoon out portions, ensuring you get plenty of the molten chocolate sauce that will have formed in the bottom. Delicious served with cream, ice cream, gooey caramel sauce (page 173), poached pears (page 39), fresh berries or toasted nuts . . . honestly though, it's pretty good just as it is.

Use gluten-free flour for a gluten-free option.

CHEAT'S 'BAKED' cheesecakes

1 tablespoon cornflour

1 tablespoon water

½ cup (110 g) caster sugar

250 g cream cheese, roughly chopped

250 g fresh ricotta*

2 free-range eggs

1 teaspoon vanilla extract or vanilla bean paste

Topping options, to serve

Roasted nuts, crushed biscuits, fresh fruit, caramel sauce (page 173), lemon curd, chocolate ganache, crumble topping, Persian fairy floss

EXTRAS

5 × 250 ml wide-mouth preserving jars with lids, or similar

This is the holy grail of dessert recipes – a little jar of cheesecake perfection that's delicious, totally foolproof, takes less than 10 minutes to whip up, can be made up to 3 days in advance, is cooked and individually served in the same dish (hardly any washing up!), and is easily transportable should you be bringing dessert or packing up lunchboxes. I've gone with a classic vanilla cheesecake, so you can add whatever toppings your heart (stomach) desires – this is one recipe that you can make over and over again with a hundred variations, and no one would know! It's your secret recipe.

FIRST

1. Mix cornflour and water together in a small bowl until cornflour is dissolved.

2. In a high-powered blender or food processor place sugar, cream cheese, ricotta, eggs, vanilla and cornflour mixture. Process until combined. Using a spatula, scrape down sides. Process again until smooth and silky.

3. Divide mixture evenly between 5 jars, filling no more than halfway. Try not to slop mixture on the sides of the jar – a jam funnel makes this process easier. Seal with lids.

4. Place inside slow cooker, then add water until jars are two-thirds submerged. Cover and cook for 2 hours on high or 4 hours on low.

2 OR 4 HOURS LATER

5. Remove jars from slow cooker and refrigerate for a minimum of 4 hours.

When you're ready to serve, remove the jar lids and add your toppings – simple as that! Dessert and bowl all in one.

+nut free +soy free +gluten free

Serves 5
Hands-on time: 15 mins
Total slow cooker time:
2 or 4 hours + 4 hours
chilling

Make your own ricotta or buy fresh from the deli. Don't use the tubs from the dairy aisle of the supermarket – not only is the flavour not as good, it often has a watery consistency meaning the cheesecake won't set properly.

Note: Ideally, get your cheese and eggs out of the fridge and allow them to come to room temperature before starting the recipe. This isn't essential, but will make it easier to pour your cheesecake mixture into the jars.

rose-berry
coulis
(page 180) →

STICKY DATE
PUDDING
for everyone

2 cups (280 g) pitted dates

1 cup (250 ml) boiling
water

1 tablespoon flaxseed
meal*

1 teaspoon bicarbonate of
soda

½ cup (110 g) brown sugar

2 tablespoons light-
tasting olive oil + extra
for greasing

1 ½ teaspoons mixed spice

1 cup (150 g) plain flour**

2 teaspoons baking
powder

EXTRAS

2 L pudding basin or
small casserole dish
(preferably with lid)
that fits inside slow
cooker

Serves 8
Hands-on time: 10 mins
Total slow cooker
time: 5 hours + 10 mins
standing

For everyone! Because firstly, it's so moreish and delicious everyone will want a slice, and secondly, it's free of dairy, eggs, soy and nuts (also making it vegan), and you can happily sub in gluten-free flour. It's one of those desserts you can make no matter who you're feeding, and without any compromise on texture or flavour – promise. This recipe might look on the longer side, but I promise it's really quick and easy – my sister Ellen couldn't believe 'that's it?!' when she tested it for me, and proclaimed it her new go-to entertaining recipe.

FIRST

1. Place dates, water, flaxseed meal and bicarbonate of soda in a high-powered blender or food processor, stir to combine. Stand for 5 minutes.

2. Add sugar, oil and spice. Process until well combined and dates are chopped but still a little chunky, 5–10 seconds.

3. Add flour and baking powder, process on low speed until just combined. Fold any leftover flour in with a spatula.

4. Grease a 2 L pudding basin with olive oil using a pastry brush. Pour in date mixture. Give it a couple of bangs on the bench to release any air bubbles. Cover pudding with lid or foil, sealing tightly.

5. Place inside slow cooker, then add water until pudding basin is two-thirds submerged. Cover and cook for 5 hours on high.

Recipe continued over page >

Recipe continued over page >

sweet treats

+dairy free +vegan +egg free +nut free +soy free +gluten free (option)

RECIPE CONTINUED

5 HOURS LATER

6. Check a skewer inserted in the pudding comes out more or less clean – not covered in raw mixture. If needed, cover and cook for a further 30 minutes on high.

7. Once cooked, remove pudding basin from slow cooker and allow to stand for 10 minutes, then turn out onto a serving plate.

It's warm and ready to serve! Cut thick slices and serve with cream, gooey caramel sauce (page 173), poached pears (page 39), ice cream or fresh strawberries . . . or a combination. Just as good served cold, so don't stress if you're struggling to get the timing exactly right – you can make it up to 3 days in advance and store in an airtight container in the fridge.

*Flaxseed meal is simply flaxseeds (also known as linseeds) milled down to a fine powder. You can buy it pre-milled, but honestly, it's often not fresh and frankly not very nice – it's best to mill your own as needed, or mill a couple of tablespoons at a time and store in the fridge or freezer. Use a high-powered blender or coffee grinder, and remember 1 tablespoon of whole flaxseeds will come out as less than 1 tablespoon of flaxseed meal.

**Use gluten-free flour for a gluten-free option.

Perfect JAR CUSTARDS

2 cups (500 ml) full-fat milk

⅓ cup (75 g) caster sugar

300 ml pouring cream

4 free-range eggs

1 teaspoon vanilla extract or vanilla bean paste

EXTRAS

5 × 250 ml good-quality preserving jars with lids

Serves 5

Hands-on time: 15 mins

Total slow cooker time: 2 or 4 hours + 8 hours chilling

Little jars of goodness, straight from the slow cooker to the fridge to the table, all with no mess! The most perfectly set custard – rich, creamy and soft with just the right amount of hold. Just like my 'baked' cheesecakes (page 136), this dessert is going to be your new secret weapon – whip up the day before, then simply pull straight out of the fridge to serve, already portioned out, already looking pretty. No effort whatsoever, so you can continue enjoying that glass of wine. I love these jars topped with my rhubarb and strawberry compote (page 37), but really the custard is pretty delicious just as it is – maybe with a sprinkling of cinnamon, a couple of fresh raspberries or some fresh passionfruit pulp.

FIRST

1. Place milk and sugar in a saucepan over very low heat and stir until sugar is dissolved.

2. Add cream, eggs and vanilla. Use a stick blender or whisk to mix until smooth. Divide mixture evenly between jars. Seal with lids.

3. Place inside slow cooker, then add water until jars are two-thirds submerged. Cover and cook for 2 hours on high or 4 hours on low.

2 OR 4 HOURS LATER

4. Remove jars from slow cooker and refrigerate for a minimum of 8 hours before serving.

When you are ready to serve, remove the jar lids and add your toppings – simple as that! Dessert and bowl all in one.

+one pot wonder +nut free +soy free +gluten free

SELF-
SAUCING
gingerbread
PUDDING

¼ cup (55 g) caster sugar

1 cup (150 g) plain flour*

2 teaspoons baking powder

⅓ cup (80 ml) coconut milk

⅓ cup (80 ml) light-flavoured extra virgin olive oil, macadamia oil or melted coconut oil**

¼ cup (90 g) golden syrup

2 tablespoons ground ginger

2 teaspoons vanilla extract

½ cup (110 g) dark brown sugar

1 ½ cups (375 ml) hot water

EXTRAS

2 L pudding basin or small casserole dish (preferably with lid) that fits inside slow cooker

This is a spin-off of my self-saucing molten chocolate pudding (page 134), but hey, when you're onto a good thing . . . The convenience of this recipe, with only one dish to wash up, and sauce and pudding all cooked in one, is just the best. My mum calls this my 'fluff dessert', and it's not a bad description – the pudding is soft and airy, almost like a soufflé, and the sauce is sweet and decadent without being heavy. Serve up a big spoonful, add a scoop of vanilla ice cream and you are set.

FIRST

1. In pudding basin or casserole dish, place caster sugar, flour, baking powder, coconut milk, oil, golden syrup, ginger and vanilla. Using a spatula, stir until well combined, then smooth down the top of the batter.

2. Sprinkle brown sugar over the top of the batter, then pour over hot water. It's important *not* to stir at this point! Cover pudding with lid or foil, sealing tightly.

3. Place inside slow cooker, then add water until pudding basin is two-thirds submerged. Cover and cook for 3 ½ hours on high.

+one pot wonder +dairy free +vegan +egg free +nut free (option) +soy free +gluten free (option)

Serves 6

Hands-on time: 10 mins

Total slow cooker time:

3 ½ hours + 10 mins

standing

3 ½ HOURS LATER

4. Remove pudding basin from slow cooker and allow to stand for 10 minutes.

Gingerbread pudding is ready! Spoon out portions, ensuring you get plenty of the caramel sauce that will have formed in the bottom. Delicious served with cream, ice cream, poached pears (page 39), fresh berries or toasted nuts . . . honestly though, it's pretty good just as it is.

Use gluten-free flour for a gluten-free option.

**If you want to keep this recipe nut free, use olive or coconut oil.*

CREAMY MANGO
coconut pudding

400 ml can coconut cream

2 ½ cups (625 ml) water

1 cup (150 g) tapioca pearls*

½ cup (110 g) caster sugar

2 mangoes, flesh diced into 1 cm cubes

2 teaspoons vanilla extract

Serves 6
Hands-on time: 10 mins
Total slow cooker time: 2 or 4 hours

I've always loved sweet, creamy, coconut-y Asian desserts. And how good is mango? Combine the two and I'm in heaven. If you've never eaten a tapioca pudding before, it's just like custard, but fresher and lighter – perfect after a big meal. In fact, I reckon you could also enjoy this one for breakfast, just like a chia pudding! This recipe honestly couldn't be easier and also takes only 2 hours to cook, meaning it's my go-to 'last minute' slow cooker dessert . . . as much as anything in a slow cooker can ever be last minute!

FIRST

1. Place all ingredients in slow cooker, stir to combine. Cover and cook for 2 hours on high or 4 hours on low.

2 OR 4 HOURS LATER

Your pudding is ready – easy as that! Serve immediately for a warm, custard-like dessert, or ladle into individual ramekins and refrigerate until ready to serve. Once chilled, the pudding will thicken to panna cotta consistency, so it's important to pour into individual serving dishes while it's still warm. If you want to serve it warm later, add coconut milk or water to thin it out and heat on the stove, stirring frequently. Top with toasted coconut, toasted sesame seeds, whipped coconut cream, coconut yoghurt or fresh fruit – all optional.

Tapioca pearls, not to be confused with sago, are little white balls that look a bit like beanbag filling. They come from a root vegetable and are commonly used in Asian cooking. Available from the baking aisle of supermarkets, health food shops and Asian grocers. Often there's a smaller and a larger size – my recipes always use the smaller.

Caramelised RUM BANANAS

¾ cup (165 g) brown sugar

¼ cup (60 g) butter*

¼ cup (60 ml) rum

5 ripe bananas, cut into
  5 mm slices

Serves 5
Hands-on time: 10 mins
Total slow cooker time:
2 or 3 ½ hours

Simple, satisfying and so easy even the kids could make it! Although perhaps if the kids are making it, substitute the rum for water. It really is a winning combination – bananas, rum, butter and sugar, and when paired with a scoop of vanilla ice cream and toasted walnuts I'm in heaven. You can have the whole recipe done in 2 hours, so pop it on as you're pulling dinner together and sit back and relax later on.

FIRST

1. Place sugar, butter and rum in slow cooker. Cover and cook for 30 minutes on high.

2. Give everything a really good stir – this should be easy now the butter is melted. Place bananas in one layer on the bottom of the slow cooker. Cover and cook for 1 ½ hours on high or 3 hours on low.

1 ½ OR 3 HOURS LATER

Your caramelised bananas are ready! Serve with ice cream, cream, yoghurt, toasted walnuts, toasted almonds, toasted coconut, on top of pancakes . . . you name it. It doesn't keep well so best to go back for seconds and finish off the lot.

For a dairy-free and vegan option, use a plant-based butter.

+one pot wonder +dairy free (option) +vegan (option) +egg free +nut free +soy free +gluten free

No-chocolate
CHOCOLATE PUDDING

400 ml can coconut cream

½ cup (50 g) cocoa powder

3 cups (750 ml) water

¾ cup (165 g) brown sugar

2 teaspoons vanilla extract

1 cup (150 g) tapioca pearls*

Serves 6
Hands-on time: 5 mins
Total slow cooker time: 1 ½ or 3 hours

This tastes just like the little tubs of chocolate mousse you buy in the dairy aisle at the supermarket, but without the chocolate, dairy, eggs, gluten, gelatine, emulsifiers, stabilisers, vegetable gums, soy lecithin, artificial flavours or artificial colours! While it's delicious warm for dessert, my favourite option is to decant it into small glass or plastic tubs with lids and store them in the fridge, pulling them out for lunchboxes throughout the week. Just like you would with the chocolate mousse from the supermarket, only this time there's no excess packaging polluting the environment and it's cheaper! With a well-stocked pantry you'll always have the ingredients on hand to whip up a batch.

FIRST

1. Place coconut cream, cocoa powder, water, sugar and vanilla in a blender and blend until smooth. Alternatively, place in a tall jug and use a stick blender. Pour mixture into slow cooker.

2. Add tapioca pearls and stir to combine. Cover and cook for 1 ½ hours on high or 3 hours on low.

1 ½ OR 3 HOURS LATER

And you're done! Serve immediately for a warm, custard-like pudding or refrigerate until ready to serve. Once chilled, the pudding will thicken to panna cotta consistency, so it's important to pour into individual serving dishes while it's still warm. If you want to serve it warm later, add coconut milk or water and heat on the stove, stirring frequently. Top with toasted coconut, toasted sesame seeds, whipped coconut cream, coconut yoghurt or fresh fruit – all optional.

Tapioca pearls, not to be confused with sago, are little white balls that look a bit like beanbag filling. They come from a root vegetable and are commonly used in Asian cooking. Available from the baking aisle of supermarkets, health food shops and Asian grocers. Often there's a smaller and a larger size – my recipes always use the smaller.

+one pot wonder +dairy free +vegan +egg free +nut free +soy free +gluten free

I've got all bases covered in this chapter, from the chilled to the warming, from the nourishing to the naughty! In winter it's so nice to have a big pot of something sweet and delicious that everyone can ladle from at their leisure, whether it's Persian tea (page 152) or a spiced hot toddy (page 151) – the keep warm function is invaluable here. Similarly, in the warmer months I love having a batch of slow cooked ginger cordial or quince syrup in the fridge, ready to make a refreshing soda or a creative cocktail. And if I ever feel a sore throat coming on, a hot drink made of my nurturing turmeric tonic (page 155) is a must.

drinks

Sweet and spiced APPLE CIDER TODDY

1 lemon

3 cups (750 ml) apple cider

½ cup (125 ml) whisky, brandy, calvados, bourbon or rum (or more to taste!)*

2 cinnamon sticks

2 star anise

8 cloves

¼ cup (55 g) dark brown sugar

¼ cup (90 g) raw honey or maple syrup**

Makes 3 mugs
Hands-on time: 10 mins
Total slow cooker time: 4 hours

Honey-sweet, cinnamon-spiced, apples and lemons . . . it's a pretty special combination! Perfect for keeping you warm and toasty through winter, thanks in part to the generous lug of liquor! But this recipe's just too special to confine only to the cooler months – make a batch in summer, allowing all those beautiful flavours to infuse, then chill and serve over ice. Hello new favourite cocktail!

FIRST

1. Peel the rind off the lemon – you only want the bright yellow part, not the white pith. Place in slow cooker. Juice the lemon and add to slow cooker also.

2. Add cider, liquor, cinnamon sticks, star anise, cloves, sugar and honey. Cover and cook for 4 hours on low.

4 HOURS LATER

Ladle into mugs, pouring through a tea strainer to remove any spices or rind. Keep any extra in the slow cooker on the keep warm setting until you're ready for seconds.

To really amp up the spices, use cinnamon whisky or spiced rum!

**For a vegan option, use maple syrup instead of honey.*

Tip: If you're having a few friends around, this amount isn't going to cut it! Double or triple all the ingredients and follow exactly the same method. Remember you can refrigerate any that's left over and heat it up on the stove another night.

drinks

+one pot wonder +dairy free +vegan (option) +egg free +nut free +soy free +gluten free

PERSIAN TEA

6 cups (1.5 L) water

6 cardamom pods, broken open*

1 cinnamon stick, roughly broken

2 tablespoons black tea leaves or 4 black tea bags

2 tablespoons rosewater**

2 tablespoons raw honey or maple syrup***

Milk of choice – soy, almond, oat, cow's – to serve (optional)

Makes 6 mugs
Hands-on time: 10 mins
Total slow cooker time:
3 to 6 hours + 5 mins

Tea is symbolic of bringing people together and this deliciously fragrant drink with a hint of sweetness does just that – as everyone will be wanting a glass! It's actually such an easy recipe, but will really add a special touch next time someone comes to visit. It also makes a great digestif, or after-dinner drink, as the spices are soothing while the honey gives that little bit of sweetness I'm often craving after a meal. Traditionally this is served in tea glasses with a sweet something on the side – perhaps dates, raisins or even a little pastry.

FIRST

1. Place water, cardamom and cinnamon in slow cooker. Cover and cook for 3–6 hours on high (the longer you leave it, the stronger the flavour, but really this time variant is more for your convenience).

3 TO 6 HOURS LATER

2. Add tea, rosewater and honey or maple syrup, stir to combine. Cover and cook for 5 minutes on high.

3. Strain mixture through a fine sieve or tea strainer into teacups.

I prefer mine served black (as is), but you can add a splash of milk as you would any cup of tea. Keep leftovers in slow cooker on the keep warm setting for top-ups.

Use a rolling pin on a chopping board to bash open the cardamom pods.

**Buy edible rosewater (not to be confused with rosewater fragrance, which is used in cosmetics) from delis and specialty grocers. Look for products made from rose petals steeped in water, not 'rosewater essence' or anything made from 'rose flavour'.*

***For a vegan option, use maple syrup instead of honey.*

Tip: If the flavour is too strong for your liking, no problem! Simply dilute with boiling water.

+one pot wonder +dairy free (option) +vegan (option) +egg free +nut free (option) +soy free (option) +gluten free

Modern
MULLED WINE

- 6 cm knob ginger, finely grated
- 1 orange, zest finely grated
- 2 × 750 ml bottles rosé or white wine
- 2 cups (500 ml) apple or pear juice
- ⅔ cup (160 ml) crème de cassis*
- ⅔ cup (150 g) brown sugar
- 2 star anise, roughly broken

Makes 8 mugs
Hands-on time: 10 mins
Total slow cooker time: 2 hours

A fresh take on traditional mulled wine – still a sweet and spiced hot drink, but this time we're using either white wine or rosé, a kick of fresh ginger and a blackcurrant liqueur. It's surprisingly fresh and light for a hot cocktail . . . and goes down dangerously easy! Don't use your favourite bottle of wine here, just something cheap (or a bottle you've opened but aren't loving).

FIRST

1. Place all ingredients in slow cooker. Cover and cook for 2 hours on low.

2 HOURS LATER

2. Ladle wine into mugs, pouring through a fine mesh strainer to remove aromatics.

Enjoy! Keep any extra in the slow cooker on the keep warm setting until you're ready for seconds.

Crème de cassis is an inexpensive blackcurrant liqueur available from bottle shops. Not only is it great in this recipe, but you can add 2 teaspoons to a glass of sparkling wine or champagne for a French 'Kir Royale' cocktail.

Tip: Not going to drink it all in one night? No problem at all! Strain into glass bottles and store in the fridge. Reheat in a saucepan over low heat another time.

drinks

+one pot wonder +dairy free +vegan +egg free +nut free +soy free +gluten free

Nurturing
TURMERIC TONIC

8 cm knob ginger, finely grated

5 cm piece turmeric, finely grated

2 lemons, zest finely grated, juiced

4 cups (1 L) water

¾ cup (265 g) raw honey or maple syrup*

Makes 1.25 L concentrate

Hands-on time: 10 mins

Total slow cooker time: 3 hours + cooling

Spicy, warming ginger with sweet honey and zesty lemon all contribute to this nurturing turmeric elixir. Basically, it's a power-packed concentrate of flavour and goodness with so many uses – add a shot to warm water on rising, dilute with soda water for a bubbly soft drink, dilute with boiling water for a tea (and add a shot of whisky for a hot toddy!). You can use it to flavour your kombucha's second ferment. You can even mix it with equal parts olive oil, plus a pinch of salt, and you've got yourself a punchy salad dressing!

FIRST

1. Place ginger, turmeric, lemon zest and water in slow cooker. Cover and cook for 3 hours on low.

3 HOURS LATER

2. Add honey and lemon juice – don't stress if you add in the lemon pips. Stir until honey has dissolved. Allow to cool completely, then pour through a fine mesh sieve into a large jug.

Decant into glass bottles and store in the fridge for up to a week, or freeze in ice cube trays and defrost cubes as needed. To serve, dilute 1 part tonic with 6 parts water.

When buying honey look to support small-scale producers who really care about their bees – it's usually not the brands stocked in the big supermarkets! For a vegan option, swap honey for maple syrup.

+freezer friendly +one pot wonder +dairy free +vegan (option) +egg free +nut free +soy free +gluten free

BOOZY
hot choccy

4 cups (1 L) milk of
    choice – soy, almond,
    oat, cow's

100 g dark chocolate,
    buttons or roughly
    broken*

¼ cup (25 g) cocoa
    powder

½ cup (110 g) brown sugar

1 cup (250 ml) liqueur of
    choice

    Irish cream whisky,
    peppermint schnapps,
    coffee liqueur, orange
    liqueur, butterscotch
    schnapps

Serves 6
Hands-on time: 10 mins
Total slow cooker time:
2 hours

Dessert and cocktail in one! Get this recipe on right after you've served up dinner and 2 hours later you'll be relaxing with a mug of warm, chocolate-y goodness in hand. My liqueur pick is peppermint schnapps for an after-dinner mint of sorts, but lovers of chocolate orange could go the orange liqueur, or for a little caffeine hit go the coffee liqueur. One easy recipe, so many options! It is incredibly rich, so maybe opt for teacups rather than your largest mug – or not, depending on the day!

FIRST
1. Place milk, chocolate, cocoa and sugar in slow cooker. Stir to combine – no need to worry about the cocoa lumps at this point. Cover and cook for 2 hours on low.

2 HOURS LATER
2. Add liqueur. Use a stick blender or milk frother to blend until smooth and frothy, ensuring you blend in the melted chocolate that's settled on the bottom of the slow cooker.

Serve immediately, keeping any leftovers in the slow cooker on the keep warm setting, ready for top-ups.

*For a dairy-free and vegan drink, use a dairy-free dark chocolate. These are often labelled as 'vegan' or 'very dark', but you'll need to check the ingredients.

Tip: You can easily double this recipe — just double the ingredients and follow the same steps. If wanting to halve the recipe, halve the ingredients and cook for 1 ½ hours on low. You'll also need to transfer the mixture to a large jug before stick blending as you won't have enough volume in the slow cooker to blend without making a serious mess!

drinks

+freezer friendly +one pot wonder +dairy free (option) +vegan (option) +egg free +nut free (option) +soy free (option) +gluten free

PROPER CHAI

3 cups (750 ml) water

4 cups (1 L) milk of
    choice – soy, almond,
    oat, cow

6 black tea bags or
    3 tablespoons black
    tea leaves

5 star anise

2 teaspoons fennel seeds

4 cm knob ginger, finely
    grated

2 ½ teaspoons ground
    cardamom

2 ½ teaspoons ground
    cinnamon

⅓ cup (115 g) raw honey
    or maple syrup*

Serves 6
Hands-on time: 10 mins
Total slow cooker time:
3 hours

This is the real deal chai, none of those bland powders or syrups! Spicy, sweet and complex, this has all the warm 'n' fuzzies in every sip. It's worth making the full amount even if it's just for you – it's easy to reheat over the coming days.

FIRST
1. Place water, milk, tea bags, star anise, fennel seeds, ginger, cardamom and cinnamon in slow cooker. Stir to combine. Cover and cook for 3 hours on high.

3 HOURS LATER
Add honey or maple syrup and stir to dissolve. Strain mixture through a fine sieve or tea strainer. Enjoy straight away, or if you like your chai frothy, froth with a milk frother or stick blender.

For a vegan option, use a plant-based milk and maple syrup instead of honey.

Note: This recipe makes a lot – refrigerate any leftovers in glass bottles and heat up on the stove as desired.

Tip: If the flavour is too strong for your liking, no problem! Simply dilute with boiling water or warm milk.

+freezer friendly +one pot wonder +dairy free (option) +vegan (option) +egg free +nut free (option) +soy free (option) +gluten free

CELEBRATION
quince syrup

1 quince, washed and
    roughly chopped into
    2 cm pieces, skin,
    core, pips and all

2 cups (440 g) caster
    sugar

5 cups (1.25 L) water

1 lemon, halved

Makes 1 L concentrate
Hands-on time: 10 mins
Total slow cooker time:
8 hours

One of my bucket list items was to eat at Chez Panisse in Berkeley, California, and wonderfully I got to tick it off with my mum. On arrival for dinner, they served us two glasses of sparkling wine with a dash of the most beautifully delicate quince syrup – I've never forgotten it. Sweet, floral, delicious . . . neither the quince nor the wine overpowered the other, but melted together beautifully. So of course, on returning to Australia, I had to replicate it. And you know what? It needs a very long, very slow cook . . . perfect for the slow cooker! It really is dead easy – you don't even need to peel or core the quince, just chop up the whole lot. It makes a litre and you only use a tablespoon per glass, so it'll last you ages, but that's perfect as quinces are only in season for a short stint during autumn. That's the time to make this recipe and then either refrigerate or freeze it to last you throughout the year. Pull it out whenever a celebration is in order and it'll feel extra special! And just between you and me, this syrup can really transform an otherwise lacklustre (aka cheap) bottle of bubbles.

FIRST

1. Place quince, sugar and water in slow cooker. Squeeze in lemon juice, pips and all, then put the entire lemon in. Cover and cook for 8 hours on high.

8 HOURS LATER

2. Place a fine mesh strainer over a large jug and ladle in quince mixture, allowing syrup to strain through but catching all solids. Refrigerate syrup until ready to serve. The quince flesh will be soft, sweet and delicious at this point – cut off the skin and enjoy with some thick cream or yoghurt.

To serve, fill champagne flutes with sparkling wine until they're almost full, then add a tablespoon of chilled quince syrup. No need to stir, just cheers and enjoy. Alternatively, use as a sweetener in cocktails or add a splash to your vodka soda. Of course, you could simply use it as a cordial – dilute with chilled water or soda.

+freezer friendly +one pot wonder +dairy free +vegan +egg free +nut free +soy free +gluten free

Classic SPICED MULLED WINE

1 orange, zest finely grated and juiced*

½ cup (110 g) brown sugar

¼ cup (60 ml) whisky

1 cinnamon stick, roughly broken

1 star anise, roughly broken

2 cloves

750 ml bottle red wine

Makes 4 mugs
Hands-on time: 5 mins
Total slow cooker time:
2 hours

While I was pretty chuffed with my modern mulled wine made with rosé or white wine (page 153), I just couldn't not include the classic version. Full-bodied, rich and heavily spiced, there's nothing better on a cold evening or around an open fire. As always with mulled wine, don't use your best bottle – save that for enjoying as is. Something cheap and cheery will do! This recipe can of course be doubled or even tripled – scale up the ingredients and follow the same steps.

FIRST

1. Place all ingredients in slow cooker. Cover and cook for 2 hours on low.

2 HOURS LATER

Ladle wine into mugs, pouring through a fine mesh strainer to remove aromatics. Enjoy! Keep any extra in the slow cooker on the keep warm setting until you're ready for seconds. Serve with a slice of orange, if desired.

If you can find a blood orange, even better!

+one pot wonder +dairy free +vegan +egg free +nut free +soy free +gluten free

drinks

FIERY GINGER *cordial*

12 cm knob ginger, finely grated*

2 cups (440 g) caster sugar

4 cups (1 L) water

Makes 1.25 L cordial
Hands-on time: 10 mins
Total slow cooker time:
3 or 6 hours

I cannot get enough of ginger! I make this cordial when I've got a bit of time and then love having it on hand for quick and refreshing sodas, spritzers and cocktails, as well as warm nurturing teas and tonics. It's great if you've got a sore throat! It'll keep for months in the fridge thanks to the sugar acting as a preservative, and you can always freeze it in ice cube trays and pull out a cube or two as needed – you're going to want it on hand all year round. While you can buy ginger year-round, the best is available at the end of autumn and the start of winter, as that's also when it's cheapest, so that's the ideal time to get a batch of this cordial on. It's also really easy to grow it yourself in warmer climates, and once it's planted it will keep giving you ginger year after year! You can even grow it in a pot.

FIRST

1. Place ginger, sugar and water in slow cooker. Cover and cook for 3 hours on high or 6 hours on low.

3 OR 6 HOURS LATER

2. Stir up any undissolved sugar. Pour through a fine mesh sieve into a large jug. Decant into glass bottles and store in the fridge (although best to wait until the syrup is cool before you do this to prevent the hot liquid breaking the glass). The leftover ginger mixture tastes like crystallised ginger – stir through fruit compotes for a ginger kick.

To serve, dilute 1 part cordial with 8 parts water, or make it stronger for more of that fiery ginger flavour! Dilute with soda water for a ginger ale, and add a shot of vodka and a squeeze of lime for a classic Moscow Mule cocktail. Use in your second ferment kombucha, or add a shot to boiling water for a sweet and nurturing ginger tea. Store in the fridge for up to 3 months.

If you're using organic ginger, wash it well before grating and there's no need to peel. You can use a food processor or high-powered blender to grate your ginger.

drinks

+freezer friendly +one pot wonder +dairy free +vegan +egg free +nut free +soy free +gluten free

These staples are my secret weapon to creating amazing meals with very little effort, while also costing very little to make (compared with buying their supermarket equivalent!) and without the common additives and dubious ingredients. It's amazing what an impact a quality homemade sauce, yoghurt, infused oil, coulis or spice mix can have on a simple dish. You'll also be amazed at what's possible in your slow cooker and just how easy it is – from gooey caramel sauce (page 173) and coconut yoghurt (page 171) to BBQ sauce (page 169). These are investment recipes – make them when you've got a little extra time on your hands and an empty slow cooker, and enjoy the rewards for weeks to come. If you grow your own produce, you'll find some of these recipes are a great way to use up the surplus – especially tomatoes! – but if not, buy fruit and veg at the peak of their season to lock them in at their best and cheapest (find out more page 25).

staples

Super-simple PASSATA

3.5 kg very ripe Roma
   tomatoes, roughly
   chopped*

1 tablespoon fine salt

1 tablespoon brown sugar

Makes 3.5 L
Hands-on time: 10 mins
Total slow cooker time:
4 or 8 hours

This is a recipe to make in summer and autumn, when you can head to your local produce market or farmer's market and find big boxes bulging with overripe tomatoes at a steal. Not only will it be the best passata you've ever tasted, but it will be incredibly cheap to make and you'll be doing your bit for the environment and food waste. Or better yet, maybe I could inspire you to plant some tomato vines in spring? They're such a great crop to grow yourself – prolific, easy to care for and you can even grow small varieties in pots! I keep the jars from 700 ml bottles of passata I've bought in the past and continue to refill and reuse them over and over – most recipes call for 700 g of passata, so this way it's already measured for me.

FIRST

1. Place all ingredients in slow cooker. Cover and cook for 4 hours on high or 8 hours on low.

4 OR 8 HOURS LATER

2. Puree using a stick blender, food processor or blender until smooth. If using a blender or food processor you will need to do this in batches.

While still warm, pour into sterilised glass bottles and store in the fridge for 2 weeks or the freezer. Use wherever a recipe calls for passata – soups, stews, pastas, curries and more! And trust me, it'll taste much better than the purchased variety.

I really do think Roma tomatoes make the best passata, but if you've got other tomatoes on hand (especially if you've grown them yourself!) use them, no problem.

Tip: If you want to extend the shelf-life of your passata and keep it in the pantry rather than in the fridge, run it through a preserving unit.

THE *best* BBQ SAUCE

- 10 garlic cloves, diced
- ¼ cup (60 ml) extra virgin olive oil
- 1 kg ripe tomatoes, diced
- 3 Granny Smith apples, peeled, cored and roughly chopped into 4 cm pieces
- 1 cup (280 g) tomato paste
- ¼ cup (70 g) Djion mustard
- 2 tablespoons smoked paprika
- 1 tablespoon fine salt
- ½ cup (125 ml) Worcestershire sauce*
- ⅓ cup (115 g) golden syrup
- ⅓ cup (80 ml) apple cider vinegar
- 1 teaspoon liquid smoke**

Makes 2 L
Hands-on time: 15 mins
Total slow cooker time: 4 or 8 hours

This sauce is everything great BBQ sauce should be – sweet, smoky, tangy, tomatoey. Especially when meat is off the menu, this sauce adds such depth of flavour . . . no one will feel they're missing out! The flavours are dynamic on your tongue, not like the flat sugary flavour of squeezy-bottle supermarket varieties. And, for BBQ sauce, it's surprisingly low in refined sugar – the whole apples deliver the trifecta of sweetness, tang and thickener. The 1 teaspoon of liquid smoke cannot be underestimated in this recipe, it really is the icing on the BBQ sauce cake.

FIRST

1. In this order, place garlic, oil, tomatoes, apples, tomato paste, mustard, paprika, salt, Worcestershire sauce, golden syrup and vinegar in slow cooker. Cover and cook for 4 hours on high or 8 hours on low.

4 OR 8 HOURS LATER

2. Add liquid smoke. Puree using a stick blender, food processor or blender until smooth. If using a blender or food processor you will need to do this in batches.

Pour into warm, sterilised jars and allow to cool completely before serving or refrigerating. Store in the fridge for up to 6 months, or run through a preserving unit if you want to store it at room temperature.

For this recipe to be vegetarian and vegan, look for an anchovy-free Worcestershire sauce, or better yet, make your own!

**Liquid smoke is one of my favourite ingredients for creating big, complex, meaty flavours without the meat – or the work! It's literally smoke in water. A single 250 ml bottle will last you forever as you only use a tiny bit at a time, and you always add it at the end of cooking to preserve the flavour. I also use it to make my facon (fake bacon)! Available online.*

+freezer friendly +one pot wonder +dairy free +vegan +egg free +nut free +soy free +gluten free

Foolproof COCONUT YOGHURT

400 ml can organic coconut cream

2 tablespoons powdered kuzu*

2 tablespoons good-quality, unflavoured, unsweetened coconut yoghurt or dairy yoghurt**

EXTRAS
1 × 500 ml good-quality preserving jar with lid

Makes 2 cups (500 ml)
Hands-on time: 10 mins + 30 mins cooling
Total slow cooker time: 1 hour + 12–24 hours standing + 24 hours chilling

I am so excited to be sharing this recipe with you – it's a game changer! It's so much cheaper to make your own and the results are just as good, if not better! Many coconut yoghurt recipes seem to be a bit hit-and-miss – sometimes they work, sometimes they don't. There's nothing more frustrating! But I promise that, thanks to my secret ingredient, kuzu, this recipe will never let you down.

FIRST

1. Place a saucepan over medium heat. Add coconut cream and kuzu and whisk consistently until coconut cream has visibly thickened – about 5 minutes. You do not want the coconut cream to boil at any stage – turn down heat if necessary.

2. Turn off heat and allow coconut cream to cool for about 30 minutes. You want it no warmer than 37°C – it should not feel warmer than body temperature to touch.

3. Once cool, add yoghurt and whisk until combined. Pour into jar and seal with lid.

4. Place jar inside slow cooker, then add water until the jar is two-thirds submerged. Cover and cook for 1 hour on low (this is one of those recipes that is very precise, it must be 1 hour only so don't let it tick over to keep warm for any length of time).

1 HOUR LATER

5. Turn off slow cooker (do not allow to tick over to 'keep warm' setting). Do not lift the lid. Leave completely undisturbed for 12–24 hours. The longer you leave it, the sourer and more yoghurty it will taste.

6. Remove jar from slow cooker and refrigerate for a minimum 24 hours.

Recipe continued over page >

+dairy free (option) +vegan (option) +egg free +nut free +soy free +gluten free

RECIPE CONTINUED

Now your yoghurt is ready to enjoy! Want it flavoured? Easy – stir through the rose-berry coulis (page 180) or tropical mango coulis (page 174). Alternatively, we can go savoury – stir through diced cucumber, olive oil, salt and lime juice for the most amazing raita (or see page 192), perfect to serve with our Mexican bean taco bowls (page 50), Loryn's lentil salad (page 126) or split peas (page 83).

*Kuzu is a Japanese starch made from the root of the kuzu plant. You'll need the powdered version for this recipe, which looks similar to arrowroot powder and is usually sold in 100 g bags. Available from Asian grocers, organic stores and my website, alycealexandra.com.

**For a true coconut yoghurt that's dairy free and vegan, use a purchased coconut yoghurt made with live bacteria (check the ingredients). However, if you've already got a good-quality dairy yoghurt (unsweetened, unflavoured) in the fridge you can use that instead. Save 2 tablespoons of this batch to use in your next one and you'll never need to buy yoghurt again!

Tip: When I make this recipe I usually double or even triple it – you can fit 4 × 500 ml preserving jars in most large slow cookers, so you can do up to 2 L. Follow exactly the same steps, just scale up the ingredients.

CHEAT'S
gooey caramel
SAUCE

2 × 395 g cans sweetened condensed milk

1 cup (250 ml) pouring cream

2 tablespoons honey

2 tablespoons golden syrup

2 teaspoons vanilla bean paste or vanilla extract

EXTRAS

2 × 500 ml good-quality preserving jars with lids

Makes 4 cups (1 L)
Hands-on time: 10 mins
Total slow cooker time: 6 or 12 hours + 8 hours chilling

Luscious, thick and easy to make, this is an incredibly rich caramel (really a dulce de leche). Bet you didn't think that was possible in a slow cooker! Drizzle over pancakes and waffles, use to frost cake or banana bread, slather between layers of a sponge, freeze in ice cream terrines, blend into milkshakes, spoon over fruit and ice cream, or incorporate into sweet pies, cheesecakes and brownies. The possibilities are endless! And you'll want to lick the spoon.

FIRST

1. Use a blender, food processor or stick blender to combine all ingredients until smooth. Pour into the two jars and seal.

2. Place jars inside slow cooker, then add water until the jars are two-thirds submerged. Cover and cook for 6 hours on high or 12 hours on low.

6 OR 12 HOURS LATER

3. Remove jars from slow cooker and refrigerate for a minimum of 8 hours. Do not disturb the caramel during this time.

Voilà! Use within 1 month (kept in the fridge) or freeze (see page 20) for longer shelf life. Totally optional, but I love serving anything caramel with a sprinkling of salt flakes.

Tip: Maybe a litre of caramel sauce seems way too much — or maybe way too little! You can make whatever quantity you like — just scale the ingredients accordingly and follow exactly the same method. In a large slow cooker you'll be able to fit four jars easily, and I figure if you're already putting a batch on, they do make pretty special edible gifts!

+freezer friendly +egg free +nut free +soy free +gluten free

Tropical mango
COULIS

4 tablespoons caster sugar

2 tablespoons lime juice

5 cups (1 kg) roughly chopped fresh mango (approximately 3 mangoes)*

EXTRAS

2 × 500 ml good-quality preserving jars with lids

Makes 4 cups (1 L)
Hands-on time: 10 mins
Total slow cooker time:
2 or 4 hours

Here we're allowing the natural beauty of the mango to shine by lightly cooking it into a chunky coulis – perfect for flavouring yoghurt (page 177), topping cheesecakes (page 136), ice cream, custard, panna cotta, granola, fruit salad . . . you name it. It couldn't be easier to do, and the cherry on top is that you don't even need to wash the slow cooker after – we both cook and store the coulis in glass jars. Pretty nifty if I do say so myself. Make the most of mangoes while they're plentiful in the warmer months and load up the freezer to add a touch of the tropics to your winter.

FIRST

1. Place 2 tablespoons sugar and 1 tablespoon lime juice in each preserving jar, then fill with as much mango as possible. Use a muddler, thin rolling pin or fork to really squash the fruit down. Leave 1 cm space at the top of the jars. Seal with lids.

2. Place jars inside slow cooker, then add water until the jars are two-thirds submerged. Cover and cook for 2 hours on high or 4 hours on low.

2 OR 4 HOURS LATER

3. Remove jars from slow cooker and allow to cool completely before refrigerating.

Use within 2 weeks or freeze (see page 20) for longer shelf life.

You can use defrosted frozen mango for this recipe, but a word of caution – packaged frozen mango can be seriously hit-and-miss as far as flavour is concerned. This recipe relies solely on mango to bring all the flavour, so taste it before using! If it doesn't taste great straight out of the packet, it's not going to taste any better after being cooked. Don't chuck it – add sparingly to smoothies.

Tip: Want to make 4 jars, or maybe only 1? No problem, just make sure you've got at least 2 tablespoons caster sugar, 1 tablespoon lime juice and 2 ½ cups (500 g) mango per jar. Follow exactly the same instructions.

+freezer friendly +one pot wonder +dairy free +vegan +egg free +nut free +soy free +gluten free

NO-JOKE *hot* SAUCE

1 red capsicum, diced

15 small red bird's eye chillies, thinly sliced*

¼ cup (55 g) caster sugar

1 teaspoon salt

3 cups (750 ml) apple cider vinegar

Makes 4 cups (1 L)
Hands-on time: 10 mins
Total slow cooker time:
4 or 8 hours

This sauce is not a joke – it's seriously fiery! When you're making hot sauce, a slow cooker is absolutely your best friend – as you slow cook the chillies they become so much more potent and intense, just what we're looking for. Traditionally served as a condiment with Mexican food, but if you love spicy food I can't see why you wouldn't also use it to add heat to soups and stews, Asian dishes . . . the works. Use very sparingly – we're talking drops! This recipe makes half a litre, which I'd say is quite a lot – perfect for decanting into little bottles and giving as edible gifts.

FIRST

1. Place all ingredients in slow cooker. Cook on high for 4 hours or low for 8 hours.

4 OR 8 HOURS LATER

2. Transfer contents to a high-powered blender. Alternatively, transfer to a tall jug and use a stick blender. Puree until smooth – keep going a bit longer than you think as you don't want the sauce to separate later.

Store in a glass bottle in the fridge for up to 6 months.

You can easily add more chilli if you're game! I used bird's eye chillies, but you can use whatever you like – often the habanero chilli is used to make hot sauce.

+freezer friendly +one pot wonder +dairy free +vegan +egg free +nut free +soy free +gluten free

Pot-set YOGHURT

- 3 ½ cups (875 ml) full-fat milk
- ⅓ cup (95 g) good-quality, unflavoured, unsweetened yoghurt*

EXTRAS

- 2 × 500 ml good-quality preserving jars with lids

Makes 4 cups (1 L)
Hands-on time: 10 mins
Total slow cooker time: 25 hours + 1 hour cooling + 24 hours chilling

Let's not ignore the elephant in the room – yes, this recipe does take nearly 51 hours. Literally. Which sounds daunting, but for 50 of them your presence is not required – the yoghurt just needs time to ferment! I am very much a lazy cook, and I promise you this recipe really is no effort at all (especially after you've made it once or twice and know what you're doing). Imagine the satisfaction of making your own pot-set yoghurt from scratch (not to mention the money you'll save and the health benefits). You've got this!

FIRST

1. Divide milk evenly between preserving jars. Seal with lids.

2. Place jars inside slow cooker, then add water until the jars are two-thirds submerged. Cover and cook for 2 hours on high.

2 HOURS LATER

3. Using tongs, carefully remove jars from slow cooker. Place the lid back on the slow cooker to preserve the heat, but turn the unit off. Set jars aside for 1 hour, or until milk has cooled to no warmer than 37°C – it should not feel warmer than body temperature to touch. Don't take too much extra time – you don't want the milk or the slow cooker to cool down to room temperature.

4. Add 2 tablespoons yoghurt to each jar, stir in well. Seal with lids.

5. Place jars back in slow cooker, cover with lid. Leave, completely undisturbed, for 24 hours (do not turn the slow cooker back on).

6. Remove jars from slow cooker and refrigerate for a minimum 24 hours.

Now your yoghurt is ready to enjoy!

Save yoghurt from this batch to use in your next one, and you'll never need to buy yoghurt again!

Tip: You can easily halve or double this recipe, making between 2 and 8 cups of yoghurt. Follow exactly the same steps, just scale up or down the ingredients.

+one pot wonder +egg free +nut free +soy free +gluten free

staples

MAGIC
pasta sauce
JARS

- 1 cup (250 g) passata*
- 4 garlic cloves, diced
- 32 basil leaves (optional)
- 4 chicken-style stock cubes or 8 teaspoons faux-chicken stock powder (page 184)
- 4 tablespoons extra virgin olive oil
- 4 tablespoons balsamic vinegar
- 1.2 kg ripe tomatoes, diced

EXTRAS
- 4 × 500 ml good-quality preserving jars with lids

Makes 2 L
Hands-on time: 10 mins
Total slow cooker time: 4 or 8 hours

Make this recipe on a Sunday afternoon when you've got a little extra time on your hands – it'll make life a whole lot easier during the week when things are crazy! Basically, it's four jars of tomato pasta sauce (often called marinara sauce) sitting in your fridge dutifully waiting for the call-up. The obvious go-to is to cook a batch of pasta, heat up the sauce and bang, you've got dinner on the table in 15 minutes. But there's so many more options! Heat up the sauce on the stove, thin down with some water or stock and add whatever veggies you've got for a nourishing soup – you can even add a can of tinned beans and you've got a minestrone! Use as sauce for a veggie bake, pasta bake, mushroom parmigiana, ratatouille . . . so many options. And (gee, I love this) there's no decanting the sauce into jars and washing the slow cooker – we cook the sauce in the jars! Magic.

FIRST

1. Divide passata and garlic between jars. In this order, add to each 8 basil leaves, 1 stock cube or 2 teaspoons stock powder, 1 tablespoon olive oil and 1 tablespoon balsamic vinegar. Divide tomatoes evenly between jars, squashing down to fit (just ensure to leave 1 cm space at the top of jar). Seal with lids.

2. Place jars inside slow cooker, then add water until the jars are two-thirds submerged. Cover and cook for 4 hours on high or 8 hours on low.

4 OR 8 HOURS LATER

3. Remove jars from slow cooker and allow to cool completely before refrigerating.

Use within a week or freeze (see page 20). Or crack one open while still warm from the slow cooker and use it straight away.

See page 167 if you want to make your own!

+freezer friendly +one pot wonder +dairy free +vegan +egg free +nut free +soy free +gluten free

Rose-berry COULIS

½ cup (110 g) brown sugar

2 teaspoons vanilla extract or vanilla bean paste

5 cups (750 g) frozen berries*

2 teaspoons rosewater (optional)

EXTRAS

2 × 500 ml good-quality preserving jars with lids

Makes 4 cups (1 L)
Hands-on time: 10 mins
Total slow cooker time: 2 ½ or 5 hours

Another one of my jar-cooked wonders! This super-simple recipe creates a sweet and juicy berry sauce that'll perfectly jazz up all manner of dishes. Flavour plain yoghurt (make your own, page 177!), drizzle over custard, ice cream, panna cotta, porridge, pancakes or fresh fruit. You can even blitz into a berry milkshake! You can use whatever berries take your fancy for this recipe (or whatever you've got in the freezer), opting for a mix or a single berry variant . . . or maybe one jar of each. The rosewater adds a nice floral touch but is by no means essential.

FIRST

1. Place ¼ cup (55 g) brown sugar and 1 teaspoon vanilla in each preserving jar, then fill with as many frozen berries as possible. Squash down to fit, leaving a space 1 cm deep at the top of the jar. Seal with lids.

2. Place jars inside slow cooker, then add water to slow cooker until the jars are two-thirds submerged. Cover and cook for 2 ½ hours on high or 5 hours on low.

2 ½ OR 5 HOURS LATER

3. Remove jars from slow cooker and wait until cool enough to touch. While still warm, open jars and add 1 teaspoon rosewater to each (if using). Mash fruit with the back of a fork until desired consistency is achieved. Replace lids and refrigerate until ready to serve.

Use within 2 weeks or freeze (see page 20).

I've used frozen berries as they're often cheaper and more accessible, but if you've got fresh – go for it! Just reduce the cooking time down to 2 hours on high or 4 hours on low.

Tip: Want to make 4 jars, or maybe only 1? No problem, just make sure you've got ¼ cup (55 g) brown sugar, 1 teaspoon vanilla, 2 ½ cups (375 g) berries and 1 teaspoon rosewater per jar. Follow exactly the same instructions.

+freezer friendly +one pot wonder +dairy free +vegan +egg free +nut free +soy free +gluten free

CHILLI *and* FENNEL SEED INFUSED OIL

4 teaspoons chilli flakes

4 teaspoons fennel seeds

500 ml extra virgin olive oil*

EXTRAS

2 × 250 ml good-quality preserving jars with lids

Makes 2 cups (500 ml)
Hands-on time: 5 mins
Total slow cooker time: 3 hours

My dear friend Angela gave me a jar of this goodness that she'd purchased from a cute local café, and I became obsessed, drizzling it on everything! What doesn't taste better with a hint of chilli and fennel? So I highly recommend you make two jars – one for yourself and one to pass on to a dear friend! Infused oils seem simple to make, but the trick is to heat the oil enough to release all the beautiful flavours, but not so much to compromise the oil! Not that easy on the stove. Here, with our friend the slow cooker, we can do a foolproof low-and-slow infusion. Brilliant.

FIRST

1. Place 2 teaspoons chilli flakes and 2 teaspoons fennel seeds in each jar, then fill with olive oil, leaving a space 1 cm deep at the top. Seal with lids.

2. Place inside slow cooker, then add water until jars are two-thirds submerged. Cover and cook for 3 hours on low.

3 HOURS LATER

Store jars at room temperature. Drizzle over salads, eggs, pasta, soups, stews . . . you name it. Make sure to scoop up some of the delicious chilli flakes and fennel seeds that will have settled on the bottom of the jar.

I highly recommend a good-quality olive oil for all cooking applications, but especially this recipe! A crappy-tasting oil is still going to taste crappy after being infused. How to tell if your olive oil is good? Have a little taste – if it tastes fresh and light, excellent, if it's bitter and leaves a fatty film in your mouth, get rid of it. If you're in Australia, always buy an Australian-grown and -pressed extra virgin olive oil.

Tip: It's not going to make any difference what size jars you use for this recipe – do it all in one big 500 ml jar or lots of really little jars. All fine. You can also do as little or as much oil as you like (I almost always do a double batch!).

+one pot wonder +dairy free +vegan +egg free +nut free +soy free +gluten free

'CANNED' BEETROOT *slices*

8 teaspoons caster sugar

2 teaspoons fine salt

8 medium beetroot, washed, ends trimmed, thinly sliced into 5 mm discs

2 cups (500 ml) white vinegar or apple cider vinegar

EXTRAS

4 × 350 ml wide-mouth good-quality preserving jars with lids

Makes 1.4 L
Hands-on time: 15 mins
Total slow cooker time:
5 or 10 hours

Just like the ones you buy, only much, much better! The flavour, honestly, cannot compare . . . these taste fresh and tangy while still maintaining all the beauty of the beetroot. Just how vegetables should be enjoyed! This recipe makes the equivalent of four cans and they can be stored for up to 6 months, so it really is one of those investment recipes you make when you've got a little extra time, and reap the rewards for months to come. You'll be thanking yourself!

FIRST

1. Place 2 teaspoons of sugar and ½ teaspoon of salt in each preserving jar. Tightly pack beetroot slices into jars – depending on the size of the beetroots you may want to cut some slices in half to fit more in. Divide vinegar evenly between jars, then top up with water, leaving a 1 cm space at the top of the jar. Seal with lids. Rotate jars on their sides to remove any trapped air bubbles.

2. Place jars inside slow cooker, then add water until the jars are two-thirds submerged. Cover and cook for 5 hours on high or 10 hours on low.

5 OR 10 HOURS LATER

Your canned beetroot is now ready! Of course, you can enjoy it hot, but it's probably best to allow it to cool for a couple of hours first. Refrigerate for up to 6 months. Add slices to salads, burgers, sandwiches, grazing platters . . . even risotto! Keep leftover beetroot liquid and use in your next batch instead of the vinegar/water mix.

+one pot wonder +dairy free +vegan +egg free +nut free +soy free +gluten free

FAUX-CHICKEN
stock powder

½ cup (200 g) fine salt*

2 tablespoons dried parsley flakes

2 tablespoons onion powder

2 tablespoons garlic powder

2 tablespoons nutritional yeast flakes**

1 tablespoon brown sugar

1 tablespoon yellow mustard seeds

2 teaspoons dried thyme

2 teaspoons celery seeds

1 teaspoon ground turmeric

Makes 2 cups
Hands-on time: 5 mins

This is one recipe that actually doesn't require a slow cooker, but I promise it will do wonders for all your slow cooking, adding big flavour with pretty much no effort! In my humble opinion it tastes better than commercial stock powders and stock cubes, and means your dinner doesn't come with a side of MSG or palm oil. And no chickens were harmed in the making of this recipe! I use this stock powder in much of this book, so make a batch when you've got a second, then add to pretty much anything and everything savoury – it makes a lot and will keep indefinitely.

1. Place all ingredients in food processor or high-powered blender until a fine powder is formed, approximately 2 minutes.

Store in an airtight jar. Use 2 teaspoons instead of your standard stock cube, or add 2 teaspoons to 500 ml water to make liquid stock.

Use a good-quality, unrefined salt such as a pink lake salt, never white table salt. This will ensure your stock powder has the best flavour and is rich in minerals such as calcium, magnesium, phosphorus, sulphur, iron, manganese, zinc and copper, not anti-caking agent.

**Nutritional yeast, commonly referred to as 'nooch', is not the same as instant yeast used in bread baking or brewer's yeast. It's a flaky yellow powder that has a cheesy, umami flavour and is packed with B12 and other vitamins and minerals. Available from health food stores and some supermarkets.*

+dairy free +vegan +egg free +nut free +soy free +gluten free

MEXICAN
spice mix

- 3 ½ tablespoons sweet paprika
- 3 tablespoons garlic powder
- 2 tablespoons onion powder
- 2 tablespoons smoked paprika
- 1 ½ tablespoons ground cumin
- 1 tablespoon chilli powder

Makes 1 cup
Hands-on time: 5 mins

Mexican food is a real crowd-pleaser and surprisingly easy to whip together in your slow cooker, especially when you've got a Mexican spice mix already on hand. There are heaps available in supermarkets, but they tend to be Mexican spices with a dose of fillers, anti-caking agents, preservatives, salt and sugar. Skip those, buy high-quality individual spices and whip up your own in no time at all! Better flavour, no additives, efficient and no doubt cheaper – winning all round!

1. Place all spices in a large jar and shake to combine, or alternatively place in a mixing bowl and stir.

Store in a sealed glass jar for up to a year. Use wherever a recipe calls for a Mexican spice blend, such as my lazy tacos (page 55) or my smoky pulled 'pork' (page 110).

Note: This recipe makes a cup, but I do use a lot of it in each recipe! So if you like Mexican, I'd recommend mixing up two or three times as much.

+dairy free +vegan +egg free +nut free +soy free +gluten free

staples

CITRUS CLEANER

(for cleaning, not eating/drinking!)

6 cups (1.5 L) white vinegar

Citrus rinds, squeezed halves and peels (equivalent to 5 pieces of fruit)*

EXTRAS

Plastic or glass trigger-spray bottle

Makes 4 cups (1 L)
Hands-on time: 5 mins
Total slow cooker time: 6 or 12 hours + cooling

This is the only recipe in the book that I don't want you to eat! This citrus cleaner is all I use to clean my kitchen at home, and I couldn't be happier with its effectiveness – it cuts through grease like nobody's business. And it'll cost you next to nothing to make, utilising citrus rinds and halves that are otherwise destined for the compost. But the best bit? My home stays chemical-free and smells fresh as a daisy – not toxic. Surprisingly, indoor air is often more toxic than outdoor air! My other fresh tip is to keep plenty of indoor plants – like trees, these purify the air and reduce moulds.

FIRST

1. Place vinegar and citrus in slow cooker. Push down to submerge the citrus as much as possible. Cover and cook for 6 hours on high or 12 hours on low.

6 OR 12 HOURS LATER

2. Ladle into a large jug or saucepan, pouring through a large fine mesh strainer to remove all remnants of citrus. Wait for vinegar to cool before decanting it into spray bottles to use around the home!

Store any leftovers in glass bottles and top up spray bottles as needed. Mist onto benchtops, stovetops, cupboards, sinks, etc., and wipe clean using a microfibre cloth. Simple as that! Just check whether acidic cleaners are suitable for your benchtops – it's advisable not to use it on granite or marble.

I never buy citrus for this recipe – I simply collect odds and ends in the fridge until I've got enough to make a batch of this cleaner. You can always store scraps in the freezer, so it doesn't matter how long it takes. You can use any combination of citrus – lemons, oranges, limes, grapefruits – just make sure to remove any stickers.

staples

+one pot wonder +dairy free +vegan +egg free +nut free +soy free +gluten free

No slow cooker required for this chapter! This section features super-simple combinations of fresh ingredients you can whip up in no time to add freshness and jazz up your slow cooker dishes. You'll see them scattered throughout this book in the serving suggestions and food shots. Food stylist and photographer Loryn (also my sister!) actually wrote these recipes – she's the queen of jazzing up dishes using fresh ingredients for both taste and aesthetic. All recipes will happily keep for a few days in the fridge and can be made in advance, so pull them together when you've got a moment and enjoy throughout the week. Herbs play the starring role in this chapter, so if you've only got the space or time to grow a couple of edibles in the garden, make it herbs! They're incredibly easy to grow, and they're so useful to have on hand, especially since you don't often need the whole bunch, leading to waste and using lots of plastic. You can even grow them in pots on a balcony or patio.

fresh accompaniments

cheat's
salsa
verde
(page 197)

fresh yoghurt
raita (page 192)

lively apple
and mint
chutney
(page 193)

zesty
zhug
(page 196)

punchy pineapple
salsa
(page 195)

no-joke
hot sauce
(page 175)

CRUNCHY CRUSHED
cucumber salad

4 Lebanese cucumbers

1 ¼ teaspoons fine salt

2 ¼ teaspoons caster sugar

2 tablespoons rice wine vinegar

1 tablespoon extra virgin olive oil

2 teaspoons toasted sesame oil*

2 teaspoons tamari or coconut aminos

1 garlic clove, diced

Chilli flakes, to taste

Small handful parsley or coriander leaves

1 tablespoon sesame seeds, fresh or toasted

Serves 4
Hands-on time: 10 mins
+ 1 hour chilling

This salad may seem a little strange – yes, I want you to bash the cucumbers! What this does is increase the surface area for the delicious dressing to soak in, and also allows the marinating process to draw out some of the moisture from the cucumbers, making the freshest, crunchiest, most cucumbery cucumber salad yet. Try it and see if you agree! Don't let the six steps fool you – it really couldn't be easier. Just make sure you start it at least an hour before you're ready to serve.

1. Cut cucumbers into quarters widthways and then into quarters lengthways. Place in a large mixing bowl.

2. Using the end of a rolling pin, smash the cucumbers until the skin starts to crack and seeds start to come apart.

3. Toss with ¼ teaspoon salt and ¼ teaspoon sugar. Refrigerate for 1 hour.

4. Meanwhile, make dressing. Place remaining 1 teaspoon salt, 2 teaspoons sugar, vinegar, olive oil, toasted sesame oil, tamari or coconut aminos and garlic in a jar and shake until salt and sugar have dissolved. Set aside to marinate.

5. Once rested, remove cucumbers from the fridge and drain off all the liquid that will now be pooling in the bottom of the mixing bowl.

6. Toss drained cucumbers in dressing, along with chilli flakes, parsley or coriander leaves and sesame seeds.

Enjoy! Your fresh cucumber salad is now ready to serve, but will happily keep in the fridge for up to 3 days. Best served chilled.

Toasted sesame oil, a mellower version of pure sesame oil, is available from health food shops. If you can't get your hands on some, just use additional olive oil.

+dairy free +vegan +egg free +nut free +soy free (option) +gluten free

Fresh yoghurt RAITA

2 Lebanese cucumbers,
   coarsely grated

2 cups coconut yoghurt*

1 lemon, juiced

1 teaspoon fine salt

Makes 4 cups
Hands-on time: 5 mins

Do not let the simplicity of this recipe fool you! It is one of my secret weapons in the kitchen – you'll see it recommended throughout this book as it's so versatile. Whip up a batch and use it throughout the week to jazz up so many different dishes, from Mexican to Indian and almost everything in between. Dollop onto Middle Eastern dishes and Greek salads, serve as an accompaniment to Indian curries and Mexican tacos, or even as a dipping sauce.

1. Mix all ingredients together – simple as that!

Refrigerate in an airtight container until ready to serve – this will happily keep for 5 days.

*Make your own! See page 171.

+dairy free +vegan +egg free +soy free +gluten free

LIVELY
apple and mint
CHUTNEY

3 long green chillies,
    quartered*

½ bunch fresh coriander

1 bunch fresh mint

2 green apples, cored
    and quartered

2 teaspoon fine salt

1 teaspoon caster sugar

1 lemon, juiced

Makes 3 cups
Hands-on time: 10 mins

My favourite way to add instant freshness, zest and a little spice to rich Indian dishes such as my chana masala (page 91), garlicky split pea dahl (page 83) and spiced Indian beetroot (page 65). I tend to keep my curries quite mild so that they suit everyone, preferring to add heat in the form of condiments that people can add to their own taste, such as this one. That keeps everyone happy, and makes the cook's job much easier!

1. Place chilli in food processer or high-powered blender and process until finely chopped.

2. Add coriander, mint and apple. Process until finely chopped, but still slightly chunky.

3. Add salt, sugar and lemon juice and mix through.

Your chutney is ready to serve! However, this will benefit from an hour to mellow, so this is a great one to make up to a couple of days in advance. Store in an airtight container in the fridge for up to 5 days.

*This recipe does pack a bit of heat – reduce the number of chillies or omit altogether if that's your taste.

+dairy free +vegan +egg free +nut free +soy free +gluten free

Punchy PINEAPPLE SALSA

1 white onion, diced into
½ cm cubes

1 pineapple, peeled,
cored and diced into
½ cm cubes

1 handful fresh parsley,
finely chopped

1 lime, juiced

½ teaspoon fine salt

½ teaspoon chilli flakes
(optional)

Makes 8 cups
Hands-on time: 10 mins
+ 1 hour marinating

Fresh, sweet, tangy and a little spicy, this is such an easy recipe to whip up and serve with anything Mexican, such as my smoky pulled 'pork' (page 110) or taco bowls (page 50). It's also an integral part of my fiesta entertaining menu (page 112). The secret is in the chopping – you want to dice the onion and pineapple as small as possible to provide little bursts of flavour throughout your dish, rather than big mouthfuls of these strong flavours! With any leftovers, toss through thinly shredded cabbage and sprinkle over broken tortilla chips and you've got yourself a fresh and delicious salad.

1. Place all ingredients in a mixing bowl and stir to combine. Allow to rest for a minimum of 1 hour before serving, but it's even better if you can leave it longer!

Keep refrigerated for up to 5 days – the lime juice lightly pickles the salsa, meaning it'll stay fresh and delicious.

Note: This recipe makes a lot – while I love leftovers, if there's only two of you this might still be too much! Simply halve the recipe – and enjoy fruit salad for dessert!

+dairy free +vegan +egg free +nut free +soy free +gluten free

ZESTY ZHUG

1 fresh jalapeño chilli, end trimmed*

2 garlic cloves, peeled

1 bunch flat-leaf parsley

1 teaspoon ground cumin

½ teaspoon ground cardamom

½ teaspoon fine salt

½ teaspoon chilli flakes (optional)

1 lemon, juiced

½ cup extra virgin olive oil

Makes 1 cup
Hands-on time: 5 mins

A fresh, bright, Middle Eastern green sauce. Similar to our salsa verde (page 197), it's fresh and zesty thanks to the fresh herbs and lemon, but this time we've got cumin and cardamom to add even more flavour. Traditionally it packs a bit of heat, but I've gone a little easy with this recipe . . . increase or decrease the spice to your taste. Drizzle over falafel, grilled vegetables, eggs, curries, roast potatoes, polenta chips (page 122), soups and stews, and even use as a dressing and toss through couscous, barley or fresh tomatoes.

1. Place jalapeño, garlic, parsley, cumin, cardamom, salt, chilli and lemon juice in a food processor or high-powered blender. Process for 5–10 seconds, until everything is uniformly finely chopped but not pureed.

2. Stir through olive oil.

Transfer to a glass jar and store in the fridge for up to a week.

Use an extra 1 or 2 jalapeños if you like spice. Any green chilli can be used for this recipe.

+dairy free +vegan +egg free +nut free +soy free +gluten free

Cheat's SALSA VERDE

1 fresh jalapeño chilli, end trimmed*

2 garlic cloves, peeled

2 big handfuls flat-leaf parsley

1 handful basil

1 handful mint, leaves picked

2 pickled cucumbers, halved**

3 tablespoons apple cider vinegar

1 tablespoon Dijon mustard

1 ½ teaspoon fine salt

½ cup extra virgin olive oil

Makes 1 cup
Hands-on time: 5 mins

There's many a recipe for salsa verde out there, but most require lots of steps and harder to come by ingredients, so we've called this one the cheat's version! Salsa verde, translating to 'green sauce', is a fresh and zesty cold sauce made predominantly of fresh herbs that's usually served with Mexican dishes, although the options don't stop there! Dip your tortilla chips in it, drizzle on tacos, nachos (page 105), refried beans, burritos, eggs, jacket potatoes (page 76) or pizza, use as a salad dressing or even as a base for a pasta sauce. It adds big flavour thanks to the fresh herbs, a hit of spice from the jalapeño and a fresh tang from the mustard and vinegar, lifting any dish.

1. Place jalapeño, garlic, parsley, basil, mint, pickled cucumber, apple cider vinegar, mustard and salt in a food processor or high-powered blender. Process for 5–10 seconds until everything is uniformly finely chopped but not pureed.

2. Stir through olive oil.

Transfer to a glass jar and store in the fridge for up to a week.

Use an extra 1 or 2 jalapeños if you like spice.

**You can find pickled cucumbers in large jars in the condiments section of the supermarket.*

fresh accompaniments

+dairy free +vegan +egg free +nut free +soy free +gluten free

ACKNOWLEDGEMENTS

Writing a book seems a little self-indulgent at times; there are so many incredibly talented, hard-working, passionate people who make a book all that it is, yet only one name goes on the front! These words can never fully encapsulate the immense contributions of others, but to each of you below, and to so many more – thank you, I am so proud of what we created together.

So much love and appreciation to everyone at Penguin Random House – our third book together and I couldn't be prouder to be a PRH author. There's so much heart in your organisation and it shows, not just in the books you produce but also in your staff. Special thanks to my dream team, Izzy and Amanda – you made this project so organised and stress-free! I really think we nailed it. And Izzy, thank you for believing in me, this book and my vision – it takes a huge leap of faith on your end to offer a book deal, and I sincerely hope I've done you proud. Louisa – you embodied my vision for this book perfectly, and I am so grateful. Tracy – you were spot-on with all your edits, polishing away while still allowing my voice to shine. And lastly, Lou – thank you for your friendship, mentoring and for championing this book right from the start. Never for a minute could I forget how important that was.

Thank you to my AA team: Sally, John, Pauline, Loryn, Ellen and Janene. Every single day you do me proud – the care and commitment each of you shows to our customers and values is the cornerstone of our success. Without our customers, none of this would exist! So a huge thank you to everyone who has my cookbooks and accessories, and everyone who has attended one of my cooking classes. It is my pleasure and privilege to serve you, and it is my mission to add value to your life. You are why I do what I do! And the fulfilment I get from knowing I've contributed positively to your life makes every long hour worth it.

Big love to Mum and Dad – just like everything I've ever done in life, I've had you two championing me the whole way. Thank you for making me believe I could do anything (like writing this book on a crazy timeline!). To my friends Ange, Tess, Tory, Poppy, Liz and Mark– thank you for all your patience, support and recipe testing! And to Claire, for proving to me just how life-changing this book could be, right when I needed the reminder.

And lastly, two very special acknowledgements for two very special people . . .

Loryn, as with everything I do, it's your magic touch that really brings it all to life. From the photos and styling, to the recipe consultation and the fresh accompaniments . . . it was all perfect in a way only you could deliver, because no one knows me better. Thank you for your love, your support and your encouragement – none of this would be possible without you.

Ellen, there's little wonder this book is dedicated to you – you were the most amazing wing-woman. You kept me going when times were tough, you kept me laughing, you kept me on schedule, you kept me focused on why this book matters. You nurtured me and the business so I could give my all to these pages, and this book is far richer for it (as are our customers!). You made sure that not for one minute was I doing it on my own, and I cannot tell you how much that meant to me.

And to you reading this – thank you for cooking, thank you for caring. We're changing the world, one meal at a time.

INDEX

VIKING

UK | USA | Canada | Ireland | Australia
India | New Zealand | South Africa | China

Viking is part of the Penguin Random House group of companies
whose addresses can be found at global.penguinrandomhouse.com.

Penguin
Random House
Australia

First published by Viking, 2021

Photography and food stylist: Loryn Babauskis
Designer: Louisa Maggio
Editor: Tracy Rutherford

Printed and bound in China by 1010 Printing International Ltd

 A catalogue record for this
book is available from the
National Library of Australia

ISBN 978 1 76089 938 7

penguin.com.au